RUSSIA
OPPOSING
VIEWPOINTS ®

Other Books of Related Interest

RUSSIA
OPPOSING
VIEWPOINTS ®

William Dudley, *Book Editor*

David L. Bender, *Publisher*
Bruno Leone, *Executive Editor*
Bonnie Szumski, *Editorial Director*
Stuart Miller, *Managing Editor*

OPPOSING
VIEWPOINTS®
SERIES

Greenhaven Press, Inc., San Diego, California

Library of Congress Cataloging-in-Publication Data

Russia : opposing viewpoints / William Dudley, book editor.
     p.   cm. — (Opposing viewpoints series)
   Includes bibliographical references and index.
   ISBN 0-7377-0522-1 (lib. bdg. : alk. paper) —
ISBN 0-7377-0521-3 (pbk. : alk. paper)
   1. Democracy—Russia (Federation) 2. Russia (Federation)—
Politics and government—1991– 3. Russia (Federation)—
Foreign relations. 4. Russia (Federation)—Economic
conditions—1991– I. Dudley, William, 1964– II. Opposing
viewpoints series (Unnumbered)

JN6699.A15 R87 2001
320.947—dc21
                                     99-086133
                                         CIP

Greenhaven Press, Inc., P.O. Box 289009
San Diego, CA 92198-9009

"Congress shall make no law...abridging the freedom of speech, or of the press."

First Amendment to the U.S. Constitution

The basic foundation of our democracy is the First Amendment guarantee of freedom of expression. The Opposing Viewpoints Series is dedicated to the concept of this basic freedom and the idea that it is more important to practice it than to enshrine it.

Contents

Why Consider Opposing Viewpoints?

"The only way in which a human being can make some approach to knowing the whole of a subject is by hearing what can be said about it by persons of every variety of opinion and studying all modes in which it can be looked at by every character of mind. No wise man ever acquired his wisdom in any mode but this."

John Stuart Mill

In our media-intensive culture it is not difficult to find differing opinions. Thousands of newspapers and magazines and dozens of radio and television talk shows resound with differing points of view. The difficulty lies in deciding which opinion to agree with and which "experts" seem the most credible. The more inundated we become with differing opinions and claims, the more essential it is to hone critical reading and thinking skills to evaluate these ideas. Opposing Viewpoints books address this problem directly by presenting stimulating debates that can be used to enhance and teach these skills. The varied opinions contained in each book examine many different aspects of a single issue. While examining these conveniently edited opposing views, readers can develop critical thinking skills such as the ability to compare and contrast authors' credibility, facts, argumentation styles, use of persuasive techniques, and other stylistic tools. In short, the Opposing Viewpoints Series is an ideal way to attain the higher-level thinking and reading skills so essential in a culture of diverse and contradictory opinions.

In addition to providing a tool for critical thinking, Opposing Viewpoints books challenge readers to question their own strongly held opinions and assumptions. Most people form their opinions on the basis of upbringing, peer pressure, and personal, cultural, or professional bias. By reading carefully balanced opposing views, readers must directly confront new ideas as well as the opinions of those with whom they disagree. This is not to simplistically argue that everyone who reads opposing views will—or should—change his or her opinion. Instead, the series enhances readers' understanding of their own views by encouraging confrontation with opposing ideas. Careful examination of others' views can lead to the readers' understanding of the logical inconsistencies in their own opinions, perspective on why they hold an opinion, and the consideration of the possibility that their opinion requires further evaluation.

Evaluating Other Opinions

To ensure that this type of examination occurs, Opposing Viewpoints books present all types of opinions. Prominent spokespeople on different sides of each issue as well as well-known professionals from many disciplines challenge the reader. An additional goal of the series is to provide a forum for other, less known, or even unpopular viewpoints. The opinion of an ordinary person who has had to make the decision to cut off life support from a terminally ill relative, for example, may be just as valuable and provide just as much insight as a medical ethicist's professional opinion. The editors have two additional purposes in including these less known views. One, the editors encourage readers to respect others' opinions—even when not enhanced by professional credibility. It is only by reading or listening to and objectively evaluating others' ideas that one can determine whether they are worthy of consideration. Two, the inclusion of such viewpoints encourages the important critical thinking skill of objectively evaluating an author's credentials and bias. This evaluation will illuminate an author's reasons for taking a particular stance on an issue and will aid in readers' evaluation of the author's ideas.

As series editors of the Opposing Viewpoints Series, it is our hope that these books will give readers a deeper understanding of the issues debated and an appreciation of the complexity of even seemingly simple issues when good and honest people disagree. This awareness is particularly important in a democratic society such as ours in which people enter into public debate to determine the common good.

Those with whom one disagrees should not be regarded as enemies but rather as people whose views deserve careful examination and may shed light on one's own.

Thomas Jefferson once said that "difference of opinion leads to inquiry, and inquiry to truth." Jefferson, a broadly educated man, argued that "if a nation expects to be ignorant and free . . . it expects what never was and never will be." As individuals and as a nation, it is imperative that we consider the opinions of others and examine them with skill and discernment. The Opposing Viewpoints Series is intended to help readers achieve this goal.

David L. Bender & Bruno Leone,
Series Editors

Greenhaven Press anthologies primarily consist of previously published material taken from a variety of sources, including periodicals, books, scholarly journals, newspapers, government documents, and position papers from private and public organizations. These original sources are often edited for length and to ensure their accessibility for a young adult audience. The anthology editors also change the original titles of these works in order to clearly present the main thesis of each viewpoint and to explicitly indicate the opinion presented in the viewpoint. These alterations are made in consideration of both the reading and comprehension levels of a young adult audience. Every effort is made to ensure that Greenhaven Press accurately reflects the original intent of the authors included in this anthology.

Introduction

"The next few years will confront Russia with a supreme test. Can the nation realize its aspirations through internal reconstruction and international cooperation, or will it once again seek to make its mark by resorting to military force and exploitation of international tensions?"
—Richard Pipes, emeritus professor of history, Harvard University

For most of the twentieth century the word Russia was often used synonymously with the Union of Soviet Socialist Republics (USSR), or Soviet Union. The Soviet Union emerged from the Bolshevik Revolution of 1917, in which Vladimir I. Lenin and his followers took over the vast but tottering Russian empire and imposed a totalitarian system of communist rule. Russia became the core of the USSR's fifteen republics. Lenin and his successors maintained and expanded the multiethnic empire they inherited, banned private property and forcibly collectivized farms (a process that resulted in the deaths of millions), and embarked on programs of rapid industrialization. The Soviet Union became a global superpower during and after World War II when it turned back Germany's attack, achieved military domination over Eastern Europe, developed atomic weapons, and engaged in a military and diplomatic competition with the United States in what became known as the Cold War. Throughout this time the Soviet Communist Party maintained a tight control over people's lives that restricted their freedoms of movement, family life, work, expression, and religion. A privileged elite of bureaucrats and party officials ran the country.

Then, following a remarkable series of events, the Soviet Union was no more. In the second half of the 1980s Soviet leader Mikhail Gorbachev introduced reforms providing greater political and economic freedoms to people that were meant to strengthen the nation's economy and revitalize public support for the communist regime. Instead, Gorbachev's reforms revealed the extent of economic stagnation in the USSR and unleashed pent-up dissatisfaction with the system. In 1990 several Soviet republics declared their independence from the Soviet Union, and the parliament of the Russian Republic declared Russian law took precedence over Soviet law. In 1991, hard-line Communists attempted to seize control of the government from Gorbachev—and failed in the face of public resistance led by newly elected Russian president Boris Yeltsin. By the end of 1991 the Soviet Union had ceased to exist and was replaced by fifteen independent states, including Russia.

Yeltsin's government inherited Moscow (the USSR's capital), three quarters of the former USSR's territory, and two-thirds of its people. However, it also inherited significant challenges in replacing the communist ideology that had provided economic and political direction over the previous decades. Columbia University political scientist Alexander J. Motyl has argued that two enormous challenges confront Russia and other former Soviet states: the need to build effective economic, legal, and political institutions from the ground up to replace the collapse of the Soviet system—and the need to do these all at the same time. Failure in one area hampers progress in another. During the 1990s Russia's new leaders sought to end state control of its economic resources, including its factories, mines, and farms, and replace them by a system of private ownership. At the same time Russia's system of laws and government had to be reformed to replace the pervasive control of the now-defunct Soviet Communist Party. The challenge in creating a market economy *and* a democratic political system is further complicated by weaknesses in Russia's public sphere; the actual functioning of Russia's government has been severely weakened by widespread tax evasion, lawlessness, organized crime, capital flight, and political corruption. While a few Russians have grown enormously rich, many have suffered from the loss of social welfare provisions of the former communist system. Russia's gross domestic product (GDP) fell to 12 percent of what was produced by the Soviet Union at its peak, according to some estimates.

The Soviet collapse also had significant repercussions for Russia's relationship with the rest of the world. Russia inherited the Soviet Red Army, most of its nuclear stockpiles,

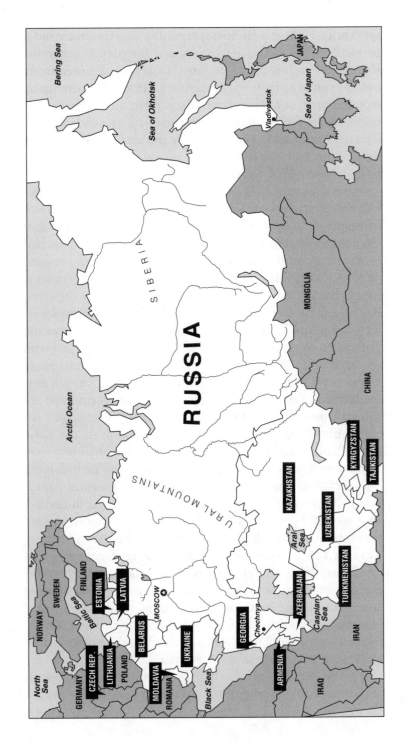

and the diplomatic ties and obligations of the Soviet Union. However, Russia's neighbors, formerly parts of the Soviet Union, are now independent states who are often fearful and hostile toward Russia. Ethnic conclaves within Russia itself—notably Chechnya—have been the site of military conflict. Russia's influence over Europe has declined, and its relationship with the United States—its ideological and military rival during the Cold War—now embraces some elements of cooperation as Russia's government seeks to embrace Western-style democracy and capitalism.

Russia's loss of its former territories and superpower prestige has not proceeded without some misgivings. "The dissolution of the Soviet Union and the loss of imperial possessions has left a mental and psychological vacuum that Russians have great difficulty filling," argues Russia expert Richard Pipes. He argues that there is a "battle for Russia's soul" between those who seek a Western model of capitalist democracy, and an older generation "suspicious of . . . Western ways and nostalgic for the more secure Soviet past." Pipes and others fear that Russia's leaders will be tempted to engage in aggressive foreign policy ventures rather than work on the difficult challenges of reforming Russia's government and economy.

Although Russia is not the superpower it once was, it remains a pivotal nation in world affairs. Russia remains the largest country in the world in surface area and in the length of its border, which stretches from Europe to Asia. It is the world's second leading nuclear power, possessing thousands of nuclear weapons. It retains a seat on the Security Council in the United Nations. Russia's geostrategic importance ensures that other nations—including the United States—will continue to have a vested interest in Russia's political and economic evolution. *Russia in Crisis: Opposing Viewpoints* examines some of the leading issues concerning Russia in the following chapters: What Are the Sources of Russia's Domestic Problems? What Are the Prospects for Democracy in Russia? Does Russia Pose a Threat to the Rest of the World? What Should U.S. Foreign Policy Be Toward Russia?

CHAPTER 1

What Are the Sources of Russia's Domestic Problems?

Chapter Preface

When Russia emerged from the collapse of the Soviet Union and communism in 1991, many people predicted a bright future for the nation. Instead, the Russian people have endured numerous hardships as the nation has attempted to transform itself from a dictatorship into a democracy and from a command economy to a market economy. Russia's gross domestic product (GDP) contracted by almost 50 percent during the 1990s. The savings of many people were wiped out by inflation and currency troubles, including a monetary crisis and devaluation of the ruble in August 1998. Sixty million people—about half the population—live below the official poverty line. Many workers have gone without a paycheck for months. The life expectancy in Russia has declined to levels comparable with some developing nations. Corruption within the government is widespread, and organized crime became an endemic and serious problem. Billions of dollars of capital have been taken from the country.

Many observers, both in and outside of Russia, have blamed reforms encouraged by the United States for Russia's economic and social difficulties. With U.S. support and assistance, the Russian government under President Boris Yeltsin removed government controls on the prices of goods, made the ruble convertible to foreign currency, and placed state-owned companies and assets into private ownership. These so-called "shock therapy" reforms have been controversial. Critics charge that they have provided more shock than therapy and have enabled an oligarchy of businesspeople, former communist officials, and organized crime figures to cheaply obtain public assets and gain a stranglehold on Russia's economy and government. Defenders of shock therapy, such as Harvard economist Jeffrey Sachs, argue that similar reforms have worked as intended in Poland and other countries, but that in Russia these reforms have not been implemented correctly or completely and have not been fully supported by other nations. The authors of the following viewpoints provide several perspectives on the origins of Russia's social and economic troubles.

"After imposing years of suffering on ordinary Russians, Russia's Western-inspired . . . program for rapidly building capitalism appears to have finally collapsed."

Capitalist Reforms Created Russia's Economic Crisis

David M. Kotz

David M. Kotz teaches economics at the University of Massachusetts-Amherst. In the following viewpoint, he blames Russia's economic difficulties, including the collapse of its currency in August 1998, on economic reforms made beginning in 1991 by the government of President Boris Yeltsin. He argues that Yeltsin's reforms—abolishing central planning, reducing public spending, eliminating controls on imports and capital, and privatizing state enterprises—were intended to quickly replace the Communist system of the former Soviet Union with a capitalist economy. However, they have instead resulted in an economic shambles marked by massive declines in economic investment and activity and the enrichment of a small and corrupt group of insiders.

As you read, consider the following questions:

1. How have average Russians been affected by Russia's economic crisis, according to Kotz?
2. What similarities does Kotz perceive between the economic programs for Russia he supports and America's New Deal reforms during the 1930s?

Reprinted from David M. Kotz, "Capitalist Collapse: How Russia Can Recover," *Dollars and Sense*, November/December 1998. Reprinted with permission.

Russian scientists were once famous for launching the world's first space satellite. Their counterparts today survive by growing vegetables in their small yards. These are not retirees enjoying some well-deserved leisure-time gardening, but prime age workers—miners and teachers as well as scientists—trying to meet basic needs in the face of economic collapse. People go to work every day and do whatever their employer asks, yet weeks and months pass without a single paycheck. They stay on the job because at least it provides some fringe benefits, and no alternative paying job exists.

This has been the meaning of Western-inspired "reform" to a majority of public and private sector workers in Russia. But the media began calling it a crisis only in August of [1998], when Russia stopped making timely payments to Western bankers and other investors who had taken a chance on Russian bonds.

The IMF Program

After imposing years of suffering on ordinary Russians, Russia's Western-inspired "neoliberal" program for rapidly building capitalism appears to have finally collapsed under its own weight. This program was devised [in 1991] by top economic advisors to Russian President Boris Yeltsin's government, working closely with specialists from the International Monetary Fund (IMF).

Any visitor to Russia can see the effects of the IMF program. The nation's economic output has fallen by half and its investment by three-fourths since 1991, with no recovery in sight. Money is so scarce that half of economic transactions are conducted through barter. A small group of influential insiders has been handed ownership of the former Soviet Union's most valuable properties, while the majority has been plunged into poverty and hopelessness. The economic and social collapse has caused more than two million premature deaths since 1991, due to sharp increases in alcoholism, murder and suicide, infectious diseases, and stress-related ailments.

Despite the unprecedented economic depression, until recently Russian bankers kept getting richer and the stock market soared, buoyed by the lucrative trade in Russia's valuable oil, gas, and metals. Western banks helped to finance the speculative binge that drove up Russian stock prices, making it one of the world's best-performing stock markets in 1997. Then in the late spring of [1998], Russia's stock market began to fall and investors started to pull their money out of the country.

The Clinton administration, fearing that Yeltsin's government would not survive a looming financial crisis, pressed a reluctant IMF to approve a $22.6 billion emergency loan on July 13. This bailout proved unsuccessful. Four weeks later the financial crisis resumed as investors fled and Russia's government had to pay as much as 300% interest to attract buyers for its bonds.

After Washington rejected Yeltsin's desperate plea for still more money, Russia did the unthinkable: it was forced to suspend payment on its foreign debt for 90 days, restructure its entire debt, and devalue the ruble. Panic followed, as Russia's high-flying banks teetered on the edge of collapse, depositors were unable to withdraw their money, and store shelves were rapidly emptied of goods. The financial collapse produced a political crisis, as President Yeltsin, his domestic support evaporating, had to contend with an emboldened opposition in the parliament.

What Caused the Financial Crisis?

Two immediate developments turned Russia's euphoria into financial crisis. One was the growing realization that the IMF had failed to resolve the Asian financial crisis, despite huge loans and the imposition of severe economic measures (known as "structural adjustment programs") upon the suffering Asian countries. This created a ripple effect in the late spring of 1998, spreading fear of the world's "emerging markets" among international investors. Equally important was the sharp drop in oil and other raw material prices during 1998. This caused the value of Russia's oil exports, its main source of foreign currency earnings, to fall by almost half in the first six months of 1998 compared to the same period of 1997. Together, these two developments led investors to begin removing their funds from Russia.

Russia suddenly began slipping into a classic debt trap. Although the government's deficit was running at only a mod-

erately high rate of 5% of GDP, by early summer the growing flight of capital out of the country forced the government to pay rapidly escalating interest rates on the money it
borrowed to finance the deficit. To make matters worse,
Russia mainly sold very short term bonds, some coming due
in a matter of weeks after issue, which only deepened its re-
payment problem. By July, Russia's monthly interest payments exceeded its monthly tax revenues by 40%. Realizing
this was unsustainable, investors began a stampede for the
door despite the IMF's huge bailout loan.

The Real Economy

But the underlying cause of Russia's financial debacle runs
deeper than the Asian financial flu or short-term movements
in raw material prices. The ultimate cause of Russia's financial collapse is nearly seven years of free fall in its real economy. The financial sector cannot prosper indefinitely while
production of real goods and services is collapsing. . . .

At the IMF's urging, Russia rapidly dismantled its pre-existing economic system—abolishing central planning, eliminating controls on imports and capital movements, and privatizing most state enterprises. A new and effective capitalist
market system was supposed to appear rapidly through individual initiative, if only the government kept out of the way.
But in the contemporary world building a capitalist system
requires an active state role and a considerable period of time.
With its old economic system dismantled and no new one to
take its place, the economy and society descended into chaos.

The IMF also insisted that, to combat inflation, Russia
must pursue a tight fiscal and monetary policy—that is,
make sharp cuts in public spending and keep money and
credit scarce. This assured that plunging demand for goods
and services would bring on a major depression. Eventually
the Russian government found it could meet the mandatory
IMF spending reduction targets only by increasing delays in
paying workers and suppliers. Unpaid suppliers could not
pay their own workers, spreading a chain of unpaid wages
and taxes through the economy.

No amount of stern IMF moralizing about how Russia
must start collecting taxes could succeed under such condi-

tions. For example, there has been much noise about the government's failure to force Gazprom, the privatized natural gas monopoly, to pay its enormous back taxes. But it turns out that, due to IMF-required public spending cuts, the government's unpaid gas bills exceed Gazprom's tax arrears!

The Decline of Russia's Gross Domestic Product

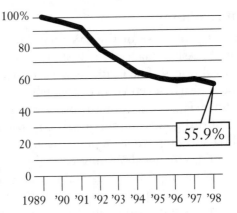

GDP index, taking 1989 as 100%

55.9%

1989 '90 '91 '92 '93 '94 '95 '96 '97 '98

Robert Dorrell, Dita Smith, and Richard Furino, *Washington Post National Weekly Edition*, September 20, 1999.

When the financial crisis struck Russia, the IMF actually insisted that the solution was more of the same—more cuts in government spending, higher taxes, and tighter credit. For a country suffering from a 50% decline in production, this is absurd advice. Any economics textbook notes that such measures, by further reducing the demand for goods and services, will only make an already severe recession worse—as President Herbert Hoover proved during 1929–32.

An Alternative Strategy

Russia's neoliberal strategy appears to have finally reached a dead end. It has failed in economic terms, and it has few supporters left in Russia—although this does not deter the Western powers from demanding that Russia "stay the course."

Advocates of the neoliberal strategy always insist that, in any event, there is no alternative.

Russia's left and center opposition has indeed developed and argued for an alternative economic strategy. Many of Russia's best economists have participated in drawing up detailed economic plans. These plans have three main principles in common: 1) the recovery of Russian industry and agriculture must take center stage; 2) the economy should be directed toward producing consumer goods for the domestic market, rather than exporting raw materials and relying on imported consumer goods; 3) the state must play an active role in economic recovery and long-run economic development instead of leaving it to the "free market."

Some specific policies that opposition groups have proposed include:

• Create a large public infrastructure investment program in transportation, power, communication, and sanitary facilities. This would both increase demand and ease supply bottlenecks.

• Immediately pay back wages to government employees, back pensions to retirees, and debts owed to nonstate enterprises for goods and services delivered to government agencies. This would facilitate payment of wage arrears by nonstate firms and would stimulate demand for Russian output.

• Steer credit away from speculation and instead provide it at low cost for productive uses in industry, construction, and agriculture.

• Renationalize those enterprises that were given away, or sold at less than true value, to influential insiders and criminal elements. This would help to establish the principle that economic reward should come from effective labor, not from insider influence.

• Increase public spending on science, technology, education, and public health. This is necessary for the long-term health and welfare of the economy and population.

• Establish temporary protection of selected domestic industries and agricultural products, to provide Russian producers an opportunity to modernize and thus compete with foreign firms on a more equal footing. It is not desirable for a large, industrialized country such as Russia to become dependent on imports for over half of its consumer goods. (Moscow food processors currently import an estimated 85% to 90% of their raw materials.)

• Redirect a major part of Russia's energy and raw materials toward use by Russian industry rather than export to the world market, while still using some primary product exports to earn foreign currency.

• Control capital flows in and out of Russia, with the aim of stopping capital flight by the oligarchy and discouraging excessive dependence on short-term foreign loans.

• Use exchange controls to redirect the foreign currency earnings from Russia's exports away from the purchase of Mercedes automobiles and other luxuries and toward products essential for the welfare of ordinary consumers and for rebuilding Russian industry.

A Russian New Deal

Apart from the renationalization plank, none of the above policies are very radical. Many of them were used at some point during the New Deal era by the U.S. government, which explains why the Russian opposition continually refers to the American New Deal as an inspiration for its program!

If Russia decisively turns away from neoliberalism and embraces a program something like the above, there is a good chance its disastrous economic collapse would be reversed, followed by economic recovery and expansion. Russia does not require Western aid or investment. It has everything it needs: abundant raw materials, an educated and skilled labor force, a diversified economic base, and a potentially large domestic market.

If Russia can be freed from the neoliberal policies that have shackled and destroyed its economic potential, it can begin to grow and develop again. Ironically, a growing Russian economy might well attract the kind of long-term foreign investors that would be helpful, although not essential, for its development. Such investors have shied away from a Russia made unstable and impoverished by seven years of neoliberal policies.

*"What Russia is actually experiencing is the
second collapse of socialist planning."*

Capitalist Reforms Did Not Create Russia's Economic Crisis

Virginia Postrel

Virginia Postrel is the editor of *Reason*, a monthly libertarian
magazine. In the following viewpoint, she takes issue with
the argument that market reforms in Russia have created an
unbridled "gangster" capitalism wreaking havoc on the nation's economy. Capitalism cannot be blamed for Russia's
economic problems, she argues, because the reforms Russia
has enacted do not add up to a real free market economy. Instead of embracing capitalism, Russia's government continues to stifle new businesses while propping up insolvent
mining and industrial operations from the Soviet era. The
result has been a sort of "pretend capitalism" that is impoverishing the nation, she concludes.

As you read, consider the following questions:

1. What analogy does Postrel make between Russia's
   economic reforms and the marital fidelity of President
   Bill Clinton?
2. What does Russia lack that prevents it from achieving
   "real" markets, in the author's view?
3. How do Russia's old industrial plants weaken its
   economy, according to Postrel?

Reprinted from Virginia Postrel, "Low Fidelity," *Reason*, November 1998.
Copyright 1998 by the Reason Foundation, 3415 S. Sepulveda Blvd., Suite 400,
Los Angeles, CA 90034; www.reason.com. Reprinted with permission.

Bill Clinton had hundreds of affairs early in his marriage, he told Monica Lewinsky, but after he turned 40 he resolved to be faithful to his wife. He cut back on his sexual adventures. Yet Clinton still committed adultery, and he still got in trouble. [Editor's note: President Bill Clinton was impeached in 1998 by the House of Representatives for offenses related to an affair he had with Lewinsky, a government intern. He was acquitted by the Senate in 1999.]

The conclusion is obvious: Fidelity is a crock, a "utopian religion," "the great illusion of our era." If it weren't for his blinkered devotion to the foolish ideology of fidelity, Clinton wouldn't be facing the possibility of impeachment.

Not even the fiercest Clinton defender would make such a ludicrous argument. No one in his right mind would claim that Clinton's reckless sexual behavior and its consequences stem from a zealous dedication to marital fidelity. And no one who offered such a patently ridiculous line would be respectfully interviewed on PBS news shows or published in the *Washington Post*.

But if you're talking about Russia, a different standard applies. It's conventional wisdom that fidelity leads to adultery.

Too Much Capitalism?

From experts both inside and outside Russia, we hear that the country's economy is falling apart because of unregulated free markets and too much reform. Leftists are ecstatic. Ever since the collapse of the Soviet Union they've been looking for a club with which to beat back the idea that markets lead to progress and prosperity. What could be better than economic turmoil in Russia? It's even the same country that made socialism look so bad.

Economics columnist Robert Kuttner puts it most rhetorically, calling the "Russian implosion" a casualty "of the great illusion of our era—the utopian worship of free markets . . . an almost lunatic credulity in pure markets and a messianic urge to spread them worldwide. . . . With serious aid, we could have helped true reformers build an effective democratic state and a modern mixed economy. Instead, the Russians got laissez-faire gangster capitalism." Markets equal the mafia.

New York University professor Stephen Cohen, a former Sovietologist and [former Soviet Union leader Mikhail] Gorbachev devotee, is more measured, as befits a man whose talking head appears regularly on PBS. But, like Kuttner, he blames Russia's troubles on an "American crusade to transform Russia into a replica of American democratic capitalism," a model he doesn't like much anyway. He says, "We have to drop this dogma about the notion that there's only one way to reform the country. Russia's changing course. . . . The state is coming back to try to save the nation." In this morality tale, the Russian state apparently withered away in 1991, taking with it all business regulations and social spending; it is only now reviving.

Now that Russia is done with its foolish experiment in free market capitalism, goes this line of argument, the country's economic policies can be pragmatic and humane. "Now there is hope for a more realistic policy," former Gorbachev economics adviser Oleg Bogomolov told the *New York Times* after the ascension of Prime Minister Yevgeny Primakov brought communists back into economic-policy positions. "Now it is not just one side that can express their ideas, like our liberal radical economists. We are all in favor of reforms, but not reforms for their own sake, but reforms which serve people."

From these accounts, and less tendentious ones as well, you might well think that Russia has been following some sort of laissez-faire model for the past seven years: that Moscow had become the new Hong Kong. Like Bill Clinton's ventures in fidelity, however, Russia's experiment with "free markets" combined a small change in behavior with a lot of good-sounding talk. In truth, Russia no more adopted a market economy—even in a mixed, social-democratic European way—than Clinton stayed faithful to his wife.

What Russia is actually experiencing is the second collapse of socialist planning. It is true that under international pressure Russia adopted "shock therapy" policies: freeing prices, privatizing some industry, and curtailing inflation. Those policies are what Cohen terms "nitwit, monetarist reforms," equating them with free markets.

But prices, sound money, and a modicum of private property do not a market economy make. They are necessary but not sufficient. The competition and feedback that distinguish real markets are missing in Russia. As economist Hernando de Soto observed of his native Peru, what shapes this economy is "bad law" and the absence of good law. Russia has loads of regulations to curtail enterprise, yet the government exercises pathetically little power to enforce contracts or punish crime. Economist Daniel Kaufmann finds that Russian senior managers or business owners must devote 30 percent to 40 percent of their time to meeting with public officials, compared to 5 percent to 10 percent in Chile or El Salvador. Bribes cost $30,000 a year for a small enterprise in Russia, and those bribes don't even reduce the time lost to meetings with officials.

Similarly, in a 1995 survey of small shop owners in Moscow and Warsaw, 76 percent of the Russians said they needed a "roof"—a private substitute for state law enforcement, providing physical protection and "dispute resolution"—to operate, compared to only 6 percent of the Poles. In Moscow, 39 percent said they'd been contacted by the criminal racket in the past six months, while only 8 percent of the Poles had. Yet the Russian officials who can't be bothered with fighting crime have plenty of time to stifle enterprise: It takes 2.71 months to register a business in Moscow vs. 0.72 months in Warsaw; Moscow shops were inspected 18.6 times in the previous year, compared to nine times in Warsaw; and 83 percent were fined vs. 46 percent in Warsaw.

Economist Andrei Schleifer, who conducted the survey with a colleague, notes that the results accord with private conversations. Russian entrepreneurs "always point to multiple permits, inspections, registrations, all requiring interactions with multiple officials many of whom need to be bribed before the necessary documents are issued. . . . To compare this to the situation in Poland, in February 1996 I asked a wealthy Polish businessman how difficult it is to open a shop in Poland. He answered immediately: 'Oh, it is very, very difficult. There are now so many shops and so much competition that it is impossible to make money.' But, I insisted, remembering my Russian conversation, 'What about permits, registrations, inspections, bribes, and other obstacles from the government?' 'These are not a problem,' answered the businessman, 'but the competition is awful; I would never recommend opening a shop in Poland.'"

From the grassroots, in other words, Russia's economy doesn't look much like a dynamic, capitalist system driven by competition and consumer choice. In a real market system, competitors—not bribe-demanding bureaucrats—drive entrepreneurs crazy.

Small shops may have to fight bureaucrats and crime lords, but at least they produce value for customers. The heavy industry that still makes up a huge proportion of the Russian economy, and employs many Russian workers, does not. It survives because Russia's economy is still run on socialist lines, with investment decisions made to serve centralized political power rather than decentralized economic competition.

Back in 1990, during the glasnost era, Soviet economist Victor Belkin told Americans that the Soviet gross national product was at best 28 percent of U.S. GNP, about half the Central Intelligence Agency's estimate. Once you factored in waste and extremely low-quality goods, he said, the Soviet standard of living was about that of China, much lower than U.S. analysts had believed. Although this estimate and others like it made a splash at the time, American commentators never really internalized the idea that Russians were as poor as Chinese, or that GNP estimates were way off. In a sense, neither did the Russians themselves.

Like the old Soviet economy, the new Russian one pretends to be larger and stronger than it is. On paper, everything looks worth much more than its real value. In Russia's old mining and manufacturing sectors, prices are arbitrary, indicating nothing about the market value of the product or labor. These "prices" work only because bills are paid in barter or not at all.

Russia's Virtual Economy

Resources do not move from wealth-destroying enterprises into wealth-creating ones. Failing businesses do not disappear; they merely suck resources out of the rest of the economy. Economists Clifford Gaddy and Barry Ickes note that "there were more corporate bankruptcies in the U.S. in the past four weeks than the entire last year in Russia." They have coined the term "virtual economy" to describe what has replaced Soviet socialism.

The virtual economy props up old industrial plants whose products are worth less than the labor and resources that go into making them. Through taxes and IOUs, it continually transfers wealth from the few enterprises that produce value into value-destroying businesses and government payments, such as pensions. Many of the transfers are merely promises of future payments—hence, the miners and railroad workers who strike for back wages and the unpaid pensioners and soldiers who threaten political unrest—but everyone pretends they are based on something real. This process makes Russia poorer and poorer, and its economic problems harder and harder to address. Western aid only worsens the situation, by allowing the pretense to continue.

It may be, as Gaddy and Ickes pessimistically suggest, that the virtual economy is thoroughly entrenched, that the Russian political system won't tolerate the disruptions of letting value-destroying businesses fail. Even many "young reformers" have political connections to these enterprises and to Russia's "Rust Belt," underscoring the case for pessimism. Pretend capitalism may be the rule in Russia for a long time to come, further impoverishing the nation.

It is, however, just pretend. Russia is not the Soviet Union, but neither is it an example of how markets work. To suggest that it is may sound good on TV, but it's just as ridiculous as upholding Bill Clinton as a paragon of fidelity.

"The two central goals of Russia's post-Soviet transformation—to build a democracy and market capitalism—are threatened by the absence of the rule of law."

Russia's Crime Problem Stems from Its Failure to Replace the Soviet State

David Hoffman

In the following viewpoint, David Hoffman, a journalist for the *Washington Post*, argues that the Russian government has failed to establish the rule of law, strengthen its legal institutions, and successfully revise and implement a new legal code after the fall of the Soviet Union. The resulting anarchy, Hoffman writes, has resulted in widespread corruption that has crippled the economy. It has also led to the growth of organized crime and a proliferation of criminal violence, including contract killings.

As you read, consider the following questions:

1. What anecdote does the author use to illustrate the extent of Russian lawlessness?
2. What fundamental assumption does Hoffman say Russian reformers made about the transferral of state property to private owners?
3. How have Russia's political and economic leaders flouted the law themselves, according to the author?

Reprinted from David Hoffman, "A Tradition of Corruption Continues," *The Washington Post*, September 20, 1999. Copyright ©1999 The Washington Post. Reprinted with permission.

Alexei Yablokov was driving down a dark country road one night, headed for his weekend cottage with his treasured white Opel jammed full of food and books, when suddenly car thieves tried to run him off the road.

They rammed his car and shouted, but Yablokov sped faster. After a harrowing chase—at one point the thieves jumped onto his hood—the white-bearded environmentalist made it safely to the cottage and called police.

But even a career spent challenging Russian authorities on nuclear-waste policy and other such issues had not prepared Yablokov for what happened next. When he went to press charges, he recalls, "It was explained to us that one of the attackers is the 'little son' of one of the tycoons of criminal business" in the region.

"They nervously asked me, 'Do you have to? It's not especially serious! Let's look at it as hooliganism,'" he says. "Nothing happened. They caught [the assailants] that night, and then they let them go."

A Legal Vacuum

Yablokov's experience is a small illustration of one of the most startling failures of post-Soviet Russia: the inability to build a state based on the rule of law. Russia has yet to replace the over-arching Soviet police state with a new system, and the outcome has been a frenzied, dangerous free-for-all.

The vacuum touches almost every aspect of Russian society, from the everyday dealings of average citizens to the high-flying finance of the country's millionaires. The chaos is highlighted by current investigations in New York and Switzerland into massive illicit flows of Russian capital abroad, and allegations of money laundering and payoffs at the highest levels of the Kremlin, including the family of President Boris Yeltsin.

At issue is what kind of post-Communist society Russia is becoming. Today, according to many businessmen, politicians and analysts, the two central goals of Russia's post-Soviet transformation—to build a democracy and market capitalism—are threatened by the absence of the rule of law. Without it, they warn, Russia may be on its way down a different path, that of many other corrupt, clannish, authoritarian regimes.

The Imprint of History

Throughout its history, from the czars to the Soviet Communist Party, Russia has no tradition of the rule of law. The legacy of previous generations runs deep and includes a chasm between state and society and a heritage of arbitrary and unreachable authorities. Power was exercised ruthlessly and without recourse for its victims. Today's Russia, despite the changes of recent years, still bears the deep imprint of this history.

"We are only 10 years away from this period," says Yuri Dmitriyev, a lecturer and law professor. "This is not 800 years of the existence of the British Constitution. This is not even 200 or 300 years of democracy in Germany and France. So, we need to create a different law, with entirely new principles and approaches. But when I talk to our members of parliament, to the presidential administration about this new structure, it is very difficult. The past is in the consciousness of the people in power."

"We are coming to the end of a crossroads period," says Mark Galeotti, director of the Organized Russian and Eurasian Crime Research Unit at England's Keele University. "The window of opportunity is almost closed to create a new Russia, rather than the old one. We are pretty close to Russia losing this opportunity."

When the new Russian state was born in late 1991, it was an article of faith among reformists that if they created a nation of property owners all else would follow. They believed that if property were taken out of the hands of the state, new owners would find it in their interest to insist on a state governed by laws.

The New Property Owners

This view has turned out to be wrong. Although an estimated 70 percent of the property was transferred to private hands, the new class of property owners has been uninterested in codifying the rule of law. Many got rich by using bribery and coercion to lay claim to Russia's mines, oil refineries and factories.

Sergei Pashin, a judge, says the intense struggle over wealth actually warped the rule of law. "When everything is finally distributed in the so-called wild capitalism, then maybe they will be interested in the rule of law," he says. "But so far, it hasn't happened. So far, it's the process of redistribution, and basically . . . the law enforcement bodies are used as a club" to settle private fights.

The Problem of Corruption

When the Soviet Union first collapsed, the first worry in the West was of a Communist revanche. Then it was mass hunger. Then it was resistance to radical reform. Now, virtually to the exclusion of everything else, it is "koruptsiya"—the image of last week's Communists, yesterday's reformers and over-dressed "New Russians" amassing billions through plunder and crony capitalism. . . .

Reports about huge sums of Russian money flowing through the Bank of New York only reinforce the notion of a nation whose entire economy, Government and military have succumbed wholesale to gangsterism, greed, embezzlement, cronyism and bribery, all with a bewilderingly sophisticated manipulation of global monetary mechanisms. . . .

Indeed, the figures for Russia offer little hope for reform anytime soon. One one side, the value of the country's resources is staggering—the value of oil alone is estimated at $30 trillion. The number of bureaucrats charged with managing and privatizing it already exceeds the total number of bureaucrats in the former Soviet Union. According to Anders Aslund, a Swedish economist, at least 70 percent of them take bribes.

Yet probably the strongest signal President Boris N. Yeltsin has sent to corrupt officials was to fire his first corruption fighter, Yuri Boldyrev, as soon as he began fingering allies of Mr. Yeltsin in the Moscow Mayor's office, the State Property Committee and the military.

Serge Schmemann, *New York Times*, August 28, 1999.

Georgi Satarov, head of a foundation that tracks the progress of democracy here and a former Yeltsin adviser, says the new capitalists are seeking maximum profit, regardless of the rules. "If there is the smallest opportunity to get access" to resources held by the state, he says, "it's more effective than fighting for clients. This practice is the child of this transition period. The old has been destroyed, the new hasn't been built; it's just being born. There are legal, cultural and ethical loopholes, and business takes advantage of them."

New Laws

New laws were written for the new Russia. The country has a post-Soviet Constitution, a civil code, family code and criminal code. But much remains unfinished, including the revamping of a tax system that is universally viewed as confiscatory and is widely disobeyed. The laws on criminal procedure date from 1964. A new land code—which could enshrine land ownership as private property—has been stymied by opposition from Communists.

"Russia lives not by law, but by understandings," says Yulia Latynina, an analyst at the Institute of the Economy in Transition, a reformist policy research center. "When I say not by the law, I mean not by those formal rules and regulations that are written into our Constitution and civil code, but by some informal rules, which are something in between a bandit's code and feudal code."

For example, she says, on the Kamchatka Peninsula in Russia's Far East, regional officials issue quota permits for catching fish, the only local commodity of value. Formally, the permits are free, but the reality is different, she says. "I know of cases where bandits paid $2 million for a hundred-ton quota for fishing crab. It is obvious that officials are interested in being able to issue 'free' quotas; in this case they get more. The higher the level of arbitrariness is, the bigger is their profit."

Weak Institutions

Russia's legal institutions are also weak, from law enforcement to the judiciary. One day last spring, for example, businessman Andrei Yakovlev raced to his retail outlet after being told that a fire had broken out there overnight. When he reached the store, Yakovlev, a 39-year-old geologist who started a company making oils and fluids for Moscow's burgeoning auto market, found that the damage was not serious. But his inventory had disappeared.

"I saw empty shelves," he recalls. "Witnesses said the [police] loaded up several cars. Simply stolen was $50,000 to $70,000." He says it was useless to file a complaint, that nothing could be accomplished, and he felt sorry for the police and firemen. "When the official wages of these people is below the poverty level," he says, "a part of the people in these jobs have to forage."

A glaring sign of the failure of law enforcement is the proliferation of contract killings. Police have failed to solve even one of several high-profile slayings here in recent years. The victims were a journalist, a television personality, a leading reformist member of parliament and an American businessman.

After legislator Galina Starovoitova was shot to death in the stairwell of her apartment building last November [1998], President Yeltsin vowed "to do everything" to find the killers. Operation Whirlwind, a sweep inspired by outrage over the killing, yielded 5,810 arrests over a few months, but no progress has been reported toward solving the case.

Even at the top, the rule of law is weak. Dmitriyev, the law professor, says many lawyers thought it an enormous victory that the Constitutional Court was established, even if only on paper. "They did not foresee a small detail," he adds. "The mechanism of enforcement of the decisions of the Constitutional Court—it does not exist. There are court bailiffs who will beat you for not paying alimony, but there is no mechanism that will make the state obey a decision of the Constitutional Court."

Leaders Flout the Law

Russia's political and financial leaders share blame for the lawlessness by flouting laws themselves. "The central element of a rule of law state is that the rulers subordinate themselves to those laws," says Galeotti. "That's what's been lacking."

Earlier [in 1999], for example, Prosecutor General Yuri Skuratov—now suspended—issued an arrest warrant for business tycoon Boris Berezovsky on corruption charges. Shortly thereafter, the interior minister at the time, Sergei Stepashin, announced he would not honor the warrant. "I am not going to arrest Berezovsky," Stepashin said, inviting him to return from abroad for questioning. The warrant was dropped.

Yuri Luzhkov, the powerful mayor of Moscow, has ignored three rulings by the Constitutional Court against the use of the notorious *propiska*, or residence permit. In Soviet times, the propiska governed where a person could live; Russia's 1993 constitution sought to end the practice, and a federal law codified the same principle.

However, Luzhkov has stubbornly preserved the system in Moscow while changing the method. Now, a permit is available only to those willing to pay thousands of dollars to buy property or pay certain "fees."

A final roadblock to building the rule of law may be Russian unfamiliarity with the notion. Dmitriyev says Russians "do not know that it is possible to resolve anything by means of law; they are simply unaware of it. If you look at the appeals of citizens to the government, to judges, letters to the president, complaints to the human rights representative, you will find a blind belief that only authority can resolve things, not the law."

"Organized crime in Russia . . . is a direct legacy of years of all-pervasive bureaucratic control in the former Soviet Union."

Russia's Crime Problem Is a Direct Legacy of the Soviet State

Gary T. Dempsey and Aaron Lukas

Gary T. Dempsey and Aaron Lukas are policy analysts at the Cato Institute, a libertarian think tank. In the following viewpoint, they assert that Russia's organized crime epidemic does not represent an extreme form of capitalism as claimed by some observers, but is instead a direct legacy of decades of Communist government under the former Soviet Union. Many members of Russia's criminal class, they assert, are current or former government officials that have used their privileged positions to their advantage both before and after the fall of the Soviet Union in 1991. Dempsey and Lukas assert that corruption and crime can be best fought by increased privatization, tax relief, and reducing the government's role in the economy.

As you read, consider the following questions:

1. What aspects of the Soviet Communist system created Russia's organized crime problem, according to the authors?
2. What relationship do Dempsey and Lukas say exists between organized crime and the Russian government?
3. What should be the proper function of government, according to the authors?

Reprinted from Gary T. Dempsey and Aaron Lukas, "Is Russia Controlled by Organized Crime?" *USA Today* magazine, May 1999. Reprinted with permission.

Russia is experiencing an organized crime epidemic. Its Interior Ministry says there are more than 9,000 criminal organizations operating inside the country, employing nearly 100,000 people, or about the same number as the U.S. Internal Revenue Service. The Analytical Center for Social and Economic Policies, a government-sponsored think tank that reports directly to President Boris Yeltsin, estimates that four of five Russian businesses pay protection money. They also indicate that more than 8,000 Russians mysteriously have vanished from their homes, which have become lucrative pieces of real estate since the collapse of communism.

American news accounts of Russia's organized crime epidemic continue to suggest erroneously that criminal operations there are an "extreme form of capitalism." Journalist Adrian Kreye, for example, said Russia is experiencing a "Mafia capitalism" that is based on "the dollar and the law of the fist," and Reuters reported that "threats and murders have become commonplace in the wild atmosphere of post-Soviet capitalism." The *Washington Post* blurred the distinction between legitimate business and organized crime with talk of criminal "conglomerates" and "mergers."

Other observers hold that organized crime in Russia is simply an "early stage" of capitalism. "Today's corruption," maintains Cornell University professor Michael Scammell, seems "characteristic of a period of profound change and upheaval, when Russian society is in the stage of the primitive accumulation of capital." Stephen Handelman, author of *Comrade Criminal: The Theft of the Second Russian Revolution*, writes that many Russians believe "that a period of lawlessness is part of the price every society pays" for capitalist development.

Organized crime in Russia is neither a form nor a stage of capitalism. Instead, it is a direct legacy of years of all-pervasive bureaucratic control in the former Soviet Union and an economy that was forced underground.

The presence of government control everywhere in Soviet life provided the original opportunity for the institutionalization of widespread bribery and extortion. Indeed, Soviet bureaucrats could, and did, demand payment for favors for everything from drivers' licenses and consumer goods to medical care and higher education.

No Uniform Rules

Moreover, bureaucratic corruption and favor-trading meant that there were no uniform laws to live by. Russians encountered rules and requirements that varied from bureaucrat to bureaucrat and government ministry to government ministry. The result was that the U.S.S.R. functioned not under the rule of law, but under the arbitrary rule of bureaucrats.

Today, Russia is paying for its failure to establish the rule of law. Faced with rampant crime, many businesses are forced to take matters into their own hands and hire private security agents and bodyguards. One security service provider says Russian businesses have little choice but to recruit their own security forces. "They do not trust the state. If they relied on the state, then you wouldn't see them riding around Moscow in a convoy. I laugh when I see five businessmen; they usually have 25 bodyguards." Officially, there are 10,000 private guard services registered in Russia, but experts say there may be as many as three times that number.

The lack of faith in the government's ability to enforce the rule of law is not limited to the business world. In 1996, a jailed Russian mobster testified before a U.S. Senate subcommittee that Russian hockey players in the National Hockey League, including the Buffalo Sabres' Alexei Zhitnick, were targeted by the Russian mob for extortion. The witness claimed that, when Zhitnick was confronted with the Mafia's demands, he did not go to the Russian authorities. Instead, he "went to a more powerful criminal group to take care of the problem." According to Zhitnick, "The cops can't do anything. No rules. No laws." Many Russians share his bleak view of the Russian government's ability to enforce the rule of law.

The underground markets that communism created are another source of Russia's organized crime problem. Shortages of consumer and producer goods in the Soviet era provided the opportunity for additional income at all stages of commerce. Goods arriving at retail stores frequently were set aside for preferred customers who paid extra. Those who controlled the distribution of goods, housing—indeed, almost everything—often were in a position to extract additional payments from consumers. "Illegal private economic activities," according to University of California at Berkeley economist Gregory Grossman, were "a major and extremely widespread phenomenon" and, for a large part of the population, "a regular, almost daily, experience."

It is no accident, then, that many members of today's criminal class are current or former government officials. The 1960s saw crime networks forged in Russia based on the ability of the criminal underground to provide Soviet officials with consumer goods and services unavailable under the communist regime.

Infiltrating the Government

As President Mikhail Gorbachev liberalized the economy in the early 1990s, organized crime retained its links to government officials, and many former police and intelligence agents joined the Russian Mafia after the collapse of communism. Several books published inside Russia support this account. *Mafia: Unannounced Visit* by Interior Ministry official Vladimir Ovchinsky describes the intertwining of the corrupt state bureaucracy and the criminal underworld, especially during the last years of communist rule. In *Thieves in Law*, Georgy Podlesskikh and Andrei Tereshonok expose how organized crime and the Russian government are tied to each other. On the basis of internal KGB documents, they show that Soviet officials influenced and sometimes supervised organized criminal activities.

Today, no level of government is immune from criminal infiltration. Take the case of Gregori Miroshnik. Imprisoned four times, he widely was considered to be a dangerous criminal. Yet, in 1991, he somehow became the economic advisor to Russia's vice president. When asked where he found his advisors, the vice president said he was too busy and couldn't check everyone's resumé.

As one frustrated former Moscow prosecutor summarizes Russia's organized crime problem: "The main way the Mafia penetrates into the economy is via the bureaucrats. They are our main enemy. The Mafiosi are only the second enemy."

The government's reluctance to give up further economic control is the single greatest catalyst to organized crime. Indeed, many Russian businesses turn to Mafia groups to evade the excessively high taxes and overly restrictive regulations. Thus, the growing scope and power of organized crime partly is attributable to the continued existence of heavy government burdens on private economic activity. Reforming the tax regime and reducing the regulatory burden would be two of the most important steps the Russian government could take to bring its organized crime epidemic under control.

A Mafia State

[In 1994] President Boris Yeltsin, in what sounded like a cry of despair, said Russia had become the world's "biggest mafia state . . . the superpower of crime." He felt overwhelmed by the lethal mix of oligarchs, former intelligence and security officers, organized crime gangs, and corrupt Soviet-era bureaucrats who had hijacked Russia's transition from a communist command economy to a market economy. Mr. Yeltsin has launched seven major crackdowns against organized crime in seven years—all to no avail. . . .

Russia began its post-communist history as a kleptocracy, which has consolidated its power ever since, but still the Clinton administration's apologists . . . insisted that Russia's looters were the latter-day equivalent of America's 19th century "robber barons." A crucial difference was overlooked. The J.P. Morgans, Goulds, Vanderbilts and Villards made their fortunes by building railroads and new industries and creating jobs. They also reinvested their profits in the future of America, such as Thomas Edison's quest for electric light. By contrast, Russia's oligarchs and their corrupt allies in government took over state-owned industries at giveaway prices, bled them white by stripping their assets, and then stashed their loot in tax havens abroad.

Arnaud de Borchgrave, *Washington Times*, September 28, 1998.

The types of crime being committed in Russia illustrate the need for further privatization and red tape cutting. Most serious organized crime in Russia is not based on "traditional" forms of illegal activity, such as prostitution or stolen-car rings, but intertwined with state-owned enterprises and resources. "It's [a] serious economic operation," notes Igor Baranovski, a reporter for *Moscow News*, "Playing games on the exchange rate. Half-legal operations selling oil." Large-scale crime in Russia often means selling government resources that nobody really owns. Billions of dollars of government-controlled resources—everything from aluminum to gold to fishing rights—have been sold for illicit private gain.

Bureaucratic Interference

Government ownership is not the sole factor that leads to corruption. Excessive bureaucratic interference with commercial activities frequently turns otherwise legitimate businessmen into criminals. At both the federal and local levels, the Russian government levies a daunting array of license, permit, and fee requirements on commercial activity. Rather than dealing with those government-created obstacles, businessmen often choose to avoid official red tape by paying less costly and more expeditious bribes. According to the director of a large Moscow bank, government officials who issue licenses and permits "practically have a price list hanging on the office wall."

A study of neighboring Ukraine, a former Soviet-run state, found that small businesses in Kiev spent an average of $2,000 a year on such under-the-table payments, whereas official fees amounted to about $12,000. The Mafia often plays the role of middleman in these situations, facilitating transactions between businessmen and corrupt government officials.

Burdensome customs procedures have made Russia into a nation of smugglers. The *Washington Post* reported that one-quarter to one-third of Russia's foreign trade is carried out by small-time importers who travel by every means imaginable. Those "shuttle traders" routinely engage in extensive illegal activities. Quasi-legitimate shipping companies charge a fee for handling paperwork, customs negotiations, and dispensing bribes. Attempts by the federal government to stiffen customs regulations merely have resulted in a greater demand for illegal facilitation services.

During the summer of 1995, such activity was observed firsthand as one of the authors of this article traveled from Turkey to Russia on a Mafia-owned passenger bus. Except for his party, the only "passengers" on the bus were color televisions, car batteries, and friendly gun-toting mobsters. The actual border crossing consisted of a quick payoff to a uniformed official followed by a bumpy ride through a dry creek bed. On boarding the bus, the customs official cheerily announced, "Good morning, Mafia! Passports please, Mafia!" Without high tariffs and labyrinthine customs procedures, such border crossings would not be necessary.

A Threat to Capitalist Reforms

Far from being a form or stage of capitalism, organized crime in Russia is a direct threat to capitalist reforms. Widespread violence and crime have begun to generate nostalgia for authoritarian rule. Flagrant lawlessness has resulted in a resurgence of politicians who promise to reestablish order and fairness by using the brute force of government. Increased criminal activity fueled the backlash that contributed to ultranationalist Vladimir Zhirinovsky's electoral success in 1993. His platform included on-the-spot execution of criminal gang leaders by firing squad and the wholesale seizure of assets thought to belong to criminals.

Moreover, rampant theft, fraud, and extortion have rendered property rights meaningless to many Russians, and without credible property rights, ownership will not facilitate investment and economic efficiency. Economist Adam Smith made that point more than 200 years ago. Owners, he said, have strong incentives to eliminate waste and maximize the value of their property, naturally seeking "the most advantageous application of every inch of ground upon [their] estate." Insecure property rights not only remove the incentives to improve one's property, but discourage the purchase of new property. Indeed, as political scientist David Weimer clearly explains in *The Political Economy of Property Rights*, "the greater the perceived risk of losing existing property rights, the less likely the holders of those rights will be to forgo current consumption to accumulate property."

As Russia shows, excessive taxes, regulations, and state ownership of property coupled with a legacy of all-pervasive government control and an economy that was forced underground lead to rampant corruption and crime. The role of the Russian state is vital to bringing that crime under control, but it must be limited in scope. Continued privatization and liberalization will render most criminal activity unprofitable, but such reform must be accompanied by changes in the police and legal system. Russia's private businesses are plagued by the inability to enforce contracts legally; laws often are conflicting; and police departments can not be relied on to provide protection from physical harm. Russian lawmakers must clarify contract laws and develop new legislation to govern private business activity. In addition, police salaries should be raised to limit incentives for corruption.

In short, what Russia needs is not more government or less capitalism, but a greater commitment to fulfilling the core tasks of liberal governance—the prevention of harm and the protection of property rights. Just as important, privatization, tax relief, and regulatory reform must be pursued more vigorously. Continuing failure in those areas will jeopardize the long-term viability of Russia's capitalist reforms and expose it to even more financial crises.

"Pollution in Russia now threatens the health of millions of citizens and the safety of crops, water and air."

An Environmental Crisis Underlies Russia's Problems

Glenn Garelik

Glenn Garelik, a reporter who writes frequently on the environment, lived in Russia from 1993 to 1995. In the following viewpoint, he argues that Russia and other former Soviet Union states are facing an environmental crisis. He describes the serious pollution situation in Kuzbass, a coal-mining region in Siberia, and asserts that such problems are common throughout Russia. Although both past Soviet and present Russian governments have passed environmental laws, Garelik writes, these laws are routinely ignored because of corruption and the lack of government resources to enforce them.

As you read, consider the following questions:

1. What are some of the sources of pollution in the Kuzbass area, according to the author?
2. What are some of the health problems associated with pollution in Russia, according to Garelik?
3. What lesson does the Russian experience hold for the United States, in the author's opinion?

Excerpted from Glenn Garelik, "Russia's Legacy of Death," *National Wildlife*, June/July 1996. Reprinted with permission.

During nearly two years as a journalist in Russia, I craved, more than anything, fresh, clean air—that and water that I could drink straight from the tap. And more than anything among the manifold blessings of life in America, it is these that I savor now that I am home.

Certainly I had had other complaints in Moscow. A little sunlight in that perpetually bleak and cloud-covered city would have been nice. And I missed good vegetables, such as tomatoes that I didn't suspect could power a small nuclear reactor. But most of all, I longed for clean air and water.

In the former Soviet Union, where for decades the government promoted production at all costs, one of the costs the nation paid was in the purity and integrity of the environment. After living without them, I still can't get enough of such seemingly simple things as safe water.

Ironically, while I was away and looking forward to coming home to a healthier environment, Americans elected a Congress that seems bent on overturning the environmental laws and regulations that, I believe, underlie the difference between America, the Still Beautiful, and the former Soviet Union, with its harrowing environmental dangers. . . .

I had only to recall what I had seen in Russia to know what happens when environmental protection takes a backseat to industry. In the Soviet Union, environmental officials were always kept subservient to the agencies that ran the military, utilities, mines, chemical industries and metalworks. As a result, pollution in Russia now threatens the health of millions of citizens and the safety of crops, water and air.

Pollution in Kuzbass

Nowhere in my travels were the weaknesses of Soviet environmental protection more apparent than in the Kuznetsk coal-mining basin, or Kuzbass, a 37,000-square-mile swath of southwest Siberia that for most of this century has been pillaged in the name of progress for its unparalleled mineral riches. The area holds effectively bottomless stores of coal, iron, manganese and gold. For example, under Kuzbass soil lie an estimated 725 billion tons of bituminous coal—145 times the total amount of coal ever mined in the entire world.

Though coal and iron ore were discovered in the region in the 1700s, for most of its history the Kuzbass, 2,000 miles east of Moscow, has harbored only the harsh penal colonies of successive despotic regimes. Rapid development came to the area in the late 1920s, when Soviet dictator Joseph Stalin ordered a nationwide expansion of the industrial base. In southern Russia, in the basin of the Don River; in the Far North, Karelia and the Kola Peninsula; and most of all, through the Ural Mountains to Magnitogorsk and east to the Kuzbass, the state built a vast zone of mines and metallurgical combines. The only limits were time and manpower. After Stalin's death in 1953, Soviet leaders expanded the Kuzbass' growth, then went after the immense reserves of oil, gas and timber in the rest of Siberia.

The Soviet slogan was stern, and everyone knew it: "We cannot expect charity from nature. We must tear it from her." Says Valentin Naidanov, vice governor of the Kuzbass, "Like a colonial power, Moscow paid little attention to what life was like here. It just wanted coal, coal, more coal." Today, both local people and the powers in Moscow must bear the results.

Life in the Kuzbass, as in the rest of the country, was organized around work. In Novokuznetsk, Russia's biggest metallurgical center after Magnitogorsk (just two of Novokuznetsk's hundreds of metalworks employ more than 70,000 of the city's 620,000 residents), the football stadium is called the Metal Worker. In Kemerovo, the regional capital and the center for coking, chemicals, dyes and fertilizers, the stadium is called the Chemist.

In a bitter irony from the Soviet era, billboards standing in soot-blackened snow along Kemerovo's main thoroughfare, still called Soviet Street, commemorate the victory over Germany in 1945 and proclaim "Glory to Labor!" In the 50 years since, the industrial hands of the victors have wrought devastation of their own.

Water Pollution

Nothing better illustrates the extent of that devastation than the River Tom, which rises in the snowy peaks that separate Russia from Mongolia and runs for 500 miles through the

Kuzbass before flowing into the Ob, one of Siberia's trio of great rivers. The Kuzbass covers just 4 percent of Siberia's territory but is home to 22 percent of Siberia's people, drawn there by industrial work. Nine out of ten of them live in a narrow north-south strip along the Tom, which is lined with some of Russia's grimiest factories. As it flows through Kemerovo, the river serves both as the city's only source of drinking water and as its sole sewer.

The Tom collects sewage and industrial waste for most of its length. In winter, hot clouds billow above the edges of the icy river—hints of the 4.8 million tons of poisons that industry dumps into the Tom each year. Carcinogenic benzene and petroleum products in the Tom average two to three times the government's legal level, according to a recent study, and during the spring thaw exceed it 15-fold. Formaldehyde measures 34 times the permissible load.

According to Yuri Kaznin, who heads the Department of Public Health of the Kemerovo Medical Institute, the river contains as much as 48 times the legal level of bacteria, 40 times the arsenic and as much as 8.5 times the phenol, a poison derived from coal tar. Groundwater is even worse, he says. It contains 150 times the acceptable level of these toxic contaminants.

A journey up a tributary of the Tom leads to Leninsk-Kuznetski, home to 160,000 people. From the center of town, an hour and a half to the south of Kemerovo, smokestacks tower in every direction, and the streets are covered with coal dust and ash. Like most of the factories here, the largest of the city's nine mines are downtown. Residents take their drinking water in pails from the Inya, the local river. Because it contains more chemical waste than water, it flows even when winter temperatures drop far below freezing.

Air Pollution

A few hours further up the Tom, in Novokuznetsk, the air grows even worse. During the spring thaw, the city's mammoth metalworks mock environmental laws, releasing into the sky three or four times the maximum legal level of heavy metals. In winter and summer, the climate conspires to trap poisonous air above the city for weeks at a time. A report by the regional Health and Epidemiology Survey indicates that sulfur levels near an agglomeration plant run as high as 312 times the acceptable level. Near a 5.4 million-square-foot pharmaceutical plant, fluoride is 300 times the norm.

The Soviet Union's Nuclear Legacy

Many residents of formerly Soviet states are now learning for the first time that "factories" or military installations in their communities were making nuclear weapons, plutonium cores or uranium fuel rods.

In Russia, he [Russian physicist Alesey Yablokov] said, more than 50 cities were secret, their existence not noted on any maps and their identities known only to the residents and to top officials in the Soviet military establishment. All of these were nuclear production sites, and all, Yablokov argues, left their own horrible lasting legacies of radioactive contamination.

Some additional nuclear production sites, he said, are within the current city limits of major population centers, including Moscow.

"Nobody wants this data," Yablokov says; at least nobody now in the government. In the early years of the Boris Yeltsin government, Yablokov was the president's personal adviser on environmental issues, overseeing declassification of pollution-related documents and setting up Russia's environmental regulatory system. Now he is chairman of the independent Centre for Russian Environmental Policy.

"My government has no money to combat pollution," he says, or to test for widespread radiation. "Every new fact showing disaster demands more money. So the government still, right now, doesn't want to have good information. They can't afford it."

Laurie Garrett, *Newsday*, November 11, 1997.

Two-thirds of the city's air pollution comes not from its monster factories but from the low stacks of its centralized, and massively inefficient, coal-burning utility plants. According to municipal authorities in Novokuznetsk, the city's air averages 10 times the legal level of benzopyrene, a carcinogen found in coal. One industrial district is burdened with 48 times the legal level. On bad days, the authorities say, nitrous oxide runs 15 times the legal level, ammonium

10 times and soot 7 times. Studies around the world have implicated these pollutants in a variety of human ailments, some fatal, ranging from asthma and sore throats to cancer. By winter's end, according to a local chemist, snow on the city's streets contains 200 times the level of pollutants that the law allows.

Residents add more than 800,000 tons of solid trash and waste yearly to a dump at the center of town, near the river bank, polluting the groundwater and carrying 225 million gallons of contaminated runoff into the Tom daily—more, authorities admit, than the purification system can handle. Industries illegally dump thousands of tons of toxic waste throughout the city each year.

According to Nikolai Korolyov, executive director of the Novokuznetsk Development Fund, a group that with foreign help is trying to address the pollution problem, even the treated water has dangerously high numbers of parasites and the organisms that cause dysentery, typhoid and paratyphoid.

Partly because of air pollution and partly because of mining, says Anatoli Shmonov, head of the regional Land Reclamation Laboratory, the soil throughout the Kuzbass is ruined. In Kemerovo, for instance, it contains 22 times the permissible levels of zinc, 31 times the lead and 35 times the arsenic, a deadly byproduct of smelting.

On a paltry budget, Shmonov's laboratory is seeking ways of living with the damage—finding which vegetables, for instance, can be raised safely in which areas. The nature of the Russian diet, which consists largely of root vegetables, compounds the problem because many of these are the plants most likely to absorb poisons from the soil. North of Kemerovo, around the city of Anzhero-Sudzhensk, beets contain five times the maximum allowable lead, zinc and cadmium.

The fact that most Kuzbass coal lies at shallow depths has invited industry to turn 3,900 square miles of what was once some of Russia's most fertile topsoil into open pits and piles of coal refuse, Shmonov says. Though heavy in radon, the mining waste is used for railroad embankments and construction. When the coal from these pits has been exhausted, the earth is left so badly scarred that, during rains and the spring thaw, a sulfurous runoff acidifies the groundwater and rivers. "What we have to work with here isn't soil," says Shmonov matter-of-factly. "It is a soil-like substance, and we have to learn how to live with it."

Other Environmental Disasters

Though its extremes may stand out, the Kuzbass is not unique among the many tragedies that choke the 8 million square miles of the former Soviet Union. For example, scientists who helped develop nuclear power plants and atomic test sites acknowledge that the nuclear industry pumped billions of gallons of deadly waste into the earth—including, near three of Russia's most important rivers, an amount equal to 60 times the radiation released during the 1986 Chernobyl nuclear-power-plant accident. According to a 1994 World Bank report "virtually all" of the country's radioactive-waste storage sites fail to meet modern standards.

Due north of the Kuzbass, near the Arctic Circle, acid rain from the smelting of nickel, copper and platinum has deforested 880,000 acres, according to the Russian newspaper Izvestiya. Solid-waste processing facilities can handle barely more than a quarter of the 7 billion tons produced annually. A 1994 report by the Security Council of President Boris Yeltsin declares that three-quarters of Russia's water is unpotable. Other studies place the figure still higher.

According to Russia's Environment and Natural Resources Ministry, the country's 1.2 million miles of oil and gas pipelines experience about 1,000 spills yearly. As much as 1.5 trillion cubic feet of the gas that rises with extracted petroleum is simply burned up. ITAR-TASS, the official news agency, reported recently that in the Komi Republic alone, where a horrific 1994 oil spill dumped as much as 300 million gallons onto the tundra and into rivers, about 40 more leaks have occurred.

In the Far East, clear-cutting is out of control. More than 1,000 plant and animal species are endangered in Russia, according to the World Bank.

All of these tragedies are the result, in the words of the Security Council report, of "economics without limits"—a "perversion of the system of values."

Health Problems

The human health consequences of this inattention to the environment have been catastrophic. For reasons that Aleksei Yablokov, the head of the Security Council's environmental commission, attributes to the degraded environment, the life expectancy of men in Russia has dropped to 57.3 years, compared to 72 in the United States. In the Kuzbass, it is only 51.

According to Andrei Luzhkov, director of immunology at the Kemerovo Medical Institute, 80 percent of workers in the Kuzbass have impaired immune systems. Other studies indicate that adults in Kemerovo are more than three times as likely as people elsewhere in the country to suffer endocrine ailments and 2.7 times as likely to have chronic bronchitis. Kemerovo's children have three times the kidney and urinary-tract infections and, according to the Medical Institute's Kaznin, 2.6 times the fatal nervous-system disorders. In one of the city's particularly polluted neighborhoods, the number of retarded children is triple the national average.

Russia's health problems, like its polluted environment, are hardly confined to the Kuzbass. In Novosibirsk, to the northeast of Kemerovo, several schools have reported cardiovascular problems in all of their students. In the Kola Peninsula, near Scandinavia, fully one-fourth of the babies have heart defects or bone-marrow disorders. Not far to the south, in the town of Nadvoitsy, decades of dumping by an aluminum plant has contaminated drinking-water sources, turning the teeth of the town's children black and rotten.

In Kazakhstan, where before the Soviet empire's breakup in 1991 half the country's zinc and lead were smelted, immune system abnormalities reportedly afflict 58 percent of the children. In Uzbekistan, where the once enormous Aral Sea was deprived of water for the sake of irrigating ever larger cotton crops, winds rushing across the dried sea bed whip up dust laden with salts, pesticides and fertilizers. In Ukraine, virtually all commerce last summer [1995] was halted in the Kharkov region when a sewage-treatment system began spilling 45 million gallons of raw sewage daily into the local river.

The environmental scourge at the root of such problems shows no signs of abating. On the contrary, according to a report released by the Environment Ministry in June [1996], air pollution in the 60 to 70 largest Russian cities, where between 40 million and 50 million people live, rises several times a year to at least 10 times higher than the legal limit. As many as 60 million other people live in places where pollution yearly exceeds health standards by at least five times.

Olga Andrakhanova, who has headed the regional Environmental Protection Committee since Soviet days, laments the lack of priority that government accords the environment—although recently, she says in a great bureaucratic flourish, the committee authorized 19 new programs and 200 inspectors to make sure that industry complies with what law there is.

Russia's Environmental Laws

Ironically, in 1949 the Soviet Union passed the world's first resolution defining maximum permissible levels of toxic substances. But like the progressive Soviet Constitution, this resolution and the nation's other environmental laws were worth less than the paper on which they were written. Regulation and enforcement, write Georgetown University demographer Murray Feshbach and journalist Alfred Friendly, Jr., "amounted to another form of the old Russian practice of pokazukha, putting a false front over grubby reality. . . . At most they constituted a minor nuisance for factory managers under pressure to fulfill their plans at all costs."

Since the breakup of the Soviet Union, Russia has added still more laws to the books. But today's reality—even where the high-minded plans are not sabotaged by corruption—is that no one can afford to follow through. For instance, Andrakhanova admits that her 19 new programs and 200 inspectors have no local budget and that only half the federal money promised them actually comes through.

Laboring for decades under industrial plans that proved short-sighted and ultimately self-defeating, the Soviet behemoth fouled its own nest. The cost of recovery is incalculable, and the coffers are bare. The Russian example stands as a reminder to Americans that, over the long haul, a people who practice production without prudence may destroy or damage all that sustains them.

"*So much of the shrinking Russian population may soon be so ill that long-term solutions to the country's political, economic, and military problems will be inconceivable.*"

A Public Health Crisis Underlies Russia's Problems

Murray Feshbach

Murray Feshbach is a research professor at Georgetown University and editor of *Environmental and Health Atlas of Russia*. In the following viewpoint, he asserts that Russia faces a serious public health crisis that is only partially attributable to its environmental problems. Feshbach predicts that Russia's population is likely to decline because of deaths due to alcoholism, violence, and infectious diseases such as tuberculosis and AIDS. Russia's health emergency will seriously degrade all efforts to solve Russia's other social and economic problems, he concludes.

As you read, consider the following questions:
1. How large a decline in Russia's population does Feshbach predict?
2. Why does Feshbach believe that official figures understate the incidence of tuberculosis in Russia?
3. What factors are creating an AIDS crisis in Russia, according to the author?

Reprinted from Murray Feshbach, "Dead Souls," *The Atlantic Monthly*, January 1999. Reprinted with permission.

H ealth in Russia is even worse than most Russian and foreign commentary would indicate, and the consequences for Russian society, the Russian economy, and the Russian military will be enormous.

Environmental issues lurk behind much of the public-health problem. Radioactive contamination is rife. Chemical contamination, such as by dioxin, is largely to blame for the fact that life expectancy for both men and women in the town of Dzerzhinsk, in the region of Nizhegorodskaya, is no better than fifty years. At least until 1995 [the pesticide] DDT continued to be used, despite an announcement by the Soviet government almost three decades ago of a ban on its production and use. Bad water nationwide has led to high rates not only of bacterial dysentery but also of hepatitis and cholera. The air in Omsk is polluted; authorities two years ago distributed some 60,000 gas masks to residents. And thermal-power plants throughout the country are spewing forth carcinogens, owing to incomplete combustion. Lead emissions in Russia are about fifty times as great as those in all of the European Union. I have seen a Russian government report indicating that as a result of lead pollution in one locale, "76.5 percent of the children in the town are mentally retarded."

But even absent these environmental problems, public health in Russia would be appalling. I anticipate that an unprecedented surge in the incidence of infectious and parasitic diseases, combined with existing high levels of alcohol poisoning and violent death, will contribute to a continued lowering of life expectancy. The Russian population is likely to decline as well, by about 800,000 to a million people a year until 2010, when the total may well be no more than 138 million. Alcoholism, drug abuse, sexually transmitted diseases, malnutrition, and various chronic and infectious diseases already mean, among other things, that a third of the adult population is incapable of reproduction.

A Tuberculosis Epidemic

The incidence of tuberculosis in Russia has skyrocketed. The number of *deaths* ascribed to tuberculosis in Russia in 1996 (24,877) was almost 15 percent greater than the number of new *infections* (usually nonfatal) that year in the United States. The Russian mortality rate for tuberculosis is 16.9 per 100,000; the U.S. rate is 0.5. According to the State Statistical Agency, the number of new cases of tuberculosis that occurred in Russia in 1996 is 99,000—an official number that is in fact far too low. It is known that at least a tenth of prison inmates in Russia have tuberculosis, and that some 850,000 to one million Russians are in prison. Are these infected prisoners in the official data? For that matter, do the agency figures include the homeless, forced migrants, refugees, people living in railroad stations, people who avoid the medical establishment, and so on? I believe that the number of new cases is actually closer to 150,000 each year. And given that even ordinary pharmaceuticals are pathetically scarce, are not most of these people going to die of the disease?

If a memorandum titled "Epidemic Tuberculosis in Russia," prepared by the Ministry of the Interior and described in a *Newsday* article by Laurie Garrett, is even close to being correct, then the Russians face a bleaker future than they (or we) could have thought possible. To quote: "By the year 2000 the incidence of [tuberculosis] will increase '50 times compared with now'; mortality will increase seventy-fold; and deaths in children are expected to rise ninety-fold." If these predictions prove true, then Russian deaths attributable to tuberculosis will be more numerous than the total reported for heart disease and cancer. In 2000, according to these numbers, tuberculosis deaths in Russia will reach approximately 1.75 million, whereas I estimate that heart-disease and cancer deaths will number about 1.5 million. This says something extraordinary about the state of public health.

AIDS in Russia

HIV and AIDS cases in Russia and deaths from AIDS are also on the verge of exploding. The former Minister of Health, Tatyana Dmitriyeva, has forecast that a million Russians will be infected with HIV by 2000. Assuming that only half that many are infected and that it costs "only" $15,000 per patient per year to administer protease inhibitors, AZT, and 3TC, where is the $7.5 billion a year for these drug cocktails to be found? The answer is nowhere. AIDS patients in Russia will die.

The growing number of Russian AIDS cases reflects a sharp rise in sexual promiscuity and hard-drug use. In the past five years syphilis cases among girls who are fourteen or younger have increased thirtyfold. Chlamydia rates are said to be very high in the same age group, though very few, and likely unreliable, data are available. How sick will these children be in subsequent years? Will they be able to have children themselves? Will their children also be sick? Will they become part of Russia's growing army of drug abusers, now thought to number four to six million? Many of them, of course, will simply die young.

Russia's Health Crisis

Illness and mortality trends do not typically play a great role in world affairs. In Russia today, however, the nation's health conditions have become so degraded that it is possible to imagine these constituting an independent, and perhaps significant, constraint upon Moscow's prospects for re-attaining Great Power status. Russia's ongoing crisis in public health—and "crisis" is hardly too strong a word—is historically unprecedented: No industrialized country has ever before suffered such a severe and prolonged deterioration during peacetime. Given its particular characteristics, Russia's health decline promises to be especially difficult to reverse. Such health trends augur ill for the Russian economy—and it is economic power that must ultimately underwrite any sustained resumption of international influence for Russia.

Thus, "unnatural" as Russia's current weakness is held to be in many quarters, there is a real possibility that the country's startlingly adverse health trends will consign it to further relative economic and political decline for as much as another generation.

Nicholas Eberstadt, *Policy Review*, June/July 1999.

Here is another way of viewing the overall health situation: How many of today's sixteen-year-old males will survive to age sixty? In the United States the figure is about 83 percent. In Russia it is only 54 percent; a hundred years ago in the European part of Russia the figure was about 56 percent. Of course, many of the Russian men who survive to age sixty will be very sick.

Analysts specializing in geopolitics, economics, or the military who ignore these issues do so at the risk of over-looking Russia's most fundamental realities. So much of the shrinking Russian population may soon be so ill that long-term solutions to the country's political, economic, and military problems will be inconceivable.

Periodical Bibliography

The following articles have been selected to supplement the diverse views presented in this chapter. Addresses are provided for periodicals not indexed in the *Readers' Guide to Periodical Literature*, the *Alternative Press Index*, the *Social Sciences Index*, or the *Index to Legal Periodicals and Books*.

Anders Aslund	"Russia's Collapse," *Foreign Affairs*, September/October 1999.
Nicholas Eberstadt	"Russia: Too Sick to Matter?" *Policy Review*, June/July 1999.
Fritz Ermath	"Seeing Russia Plain," *National Interest*, Spring 1999.
Mikhail Gorbachev	"Russia Needs a Change," *Nation*, October 5, 1998.
David Hoffman	"Russia's Capital Flight Problem," *Washington Post National Weekly Edition*, September 6, 1999. Available from Reprints, 1150 15th St. NW, Washington, DC 20071.
Garry Kasparov	"Tycoons Flourish as Russia Heads for the Rocks," *Wall Street Journal*, September 1, 1998.
John Lloyd	"Who Lost Russia?" *New York Times Magazine*, August 15, 1999.
Andrew Meier	"Russia in the Red," *Harper's Magazine*, June 1999.
Thomas Nowotny	"The Russian Crisis," *Dissent*, Spring 1999.
Michael Schwellen	"Russia's Environmental Mess," *World Press Review*, February 1995.
Matt Taibbi and Mark Ames	"The *Journal*'s Russia Scandal," *Nation*, October 4, 1999.
Hillel Ticktin and Susan Weissman	"The Russian Crisis: Capitalism Is in Question," *Against the Current*, November/December 1998.
Janine R. Wedel	"The Harvard Boys Do Russia," *Nation*, June 1, 1998.
Grigory Yavlinsky	"Russia's Phony Capitalism," *Foreign Affairs*, May/June 1998.
Fareed Zakaria	"Lousy Advice Has Its Price," *Newsweek*, September 27, 1999.

CHAPTER 2

What Are the Prospects for Democracy in Russia?

Chapter Preface

On July 3, 1996, Boris Yeltsin pulled off a remarkable political comeback when he was elected to a second term as president of Russia. A prominent Communist Party official in the old Soviet Union who became an opposition figure when he was ousted from the ruling Politburo in 1988, Yeltsin had been elected president of the Russian Federation in 1991 when it was still a part of the Soviet Union. By early 1996, with a mixed record on economic reforms and an unpopular military campaign in the breakaway region of Chechnya, his approval ratings had fallen below 10 percent. But with assistance from newly enriched Russian capitalists and a group of American political operatives, Yeltsin was able to convince a majority of voters that electing his chief opponent—Communist leader Gennady Zyuganov—would be an unacceptable return to the Soviet undemocratic past.

The election was hailed by many as a triumph not only for Yeltsin, but also for Russian democracy. Most observers agreed that it had been carried out with minimal fraud and violence. After his defeat, Zyuganov sent Yeltsin a congratulatory telegram rather than calling for strikes or protests. It was a far cry from the one-candidate elections held under the old Soviet Union.

Russia held its next presidential election in March 2000. Vladimr Putin, a former spy who had been serving as acting president since Yeltsin resigned abruptly at the close of 1999, emerged victorious. Despite the successful and peaceful transfer of power from Yeltsin to his designated successor, democracy's future in Russia remains uncertain. "Free elections are necessary for democracy," states political science and Russian studies professor Stephen Cohen, "but they are not sufficient." Obstacles to a stable democracy include an insecure middle class, the lack of the rule of law, and Russia's long tradition of authoritarian rule. Critics of Yeltsin pointed to his tendency to rule by presidential decree, ignoring the legislative and judicial branches of government. Whether democracy becomes a permanent fixture in Russian society under Yeltsin's successor remains open to question. The viewpoints in this chapter examine democracy's prospects in Russia.

"What is known today as 'Russian democracy' masks a government of a completely different sort."

Russia Has Failed to Achieve True Democracy

Aleksandr Solzhenitsyn

Aleksandr Solzhenitsyn won the Nobel Prize for literature in 1970 for his books describing the cruelties of Soviet Union labor camps and prisons. One of the most famous dissidents of the Soviet era, Solzhenitsyn was expelled from the Soviet Union in 1974 and resided in the United States for twenty years. He moved back to Russia in 1994. In the following viewpoint, he argues that, for all its changes since the demise of the Soviet Union in 1991, Russia cannot be considered a true democracy in which the people rule themselves. Instead, an inept oligarchy of presidential appointees and bureaucrats has created a system of centralized power that is not accountable to Russia's citizens.

As you read, consider the following questions:
1. Why does Solzhenitsyn consider freedom of the press in Russia to be illusory?
2. What has prevented the development of local self-government, according to Solzhenitsyn?
3. What criticisms does the author have about the 1996 presidential elections in Russia?

Reprinted from Aleksandr Solzhenitsyn, "What Kind of 'Democracy' Is This?" Translated by Richard Lourie. *The New York Times*, January 4, 1997. Copyright ©1997 The New York Times. Reprinted with permission.

How does Russia look to Europe at the present moment? Usually, the attention of Western observers is not focused on Russia's overall condition and the forces at work in the country but on the latest developments, like the elections to the Duma, the presidential contest, . . . Boris Yeltsin's heart surgery. Any broad, deep view of what is happening gets lost.

As far as I can judge, two strongly held opinions are widely shared in the West: that during the last few years democracy has unquestionably been established in Russia, albeit one under a dangerously weak national Government, and that effective economic reforms have been adopted to foster the creation of a free market, to which the way is now open.

Both views are mistaken.

What is known today as "Russian democracy" masks a government of a completely different sort. Glasnost—freedom of the press—is only an instrument of democracy, not democracy itself. And to a great extent freedom of the press is illusory since the owners of newspapers erect strict taboos against discussion of issues of vital importance, while in the outlying parts of the country newspapers get direct pressure from the provincial authorities.

No Democracy in Russia

Democracy in the unarguable sense of the word means the rule of the people—that is, a system in which the people are truly in charge of their daily lives and can influence the course of their own historical fate. There is nothing of the sort in Russia today.

In August 1991, the "councils of people's deputies," though only window dressing under the rule of the Communist Party, were abolished throughout the country. Since then the united resistance of the president's machine, the government, state Duma, leaders of the political parties and majority of governors has prevented the creation of any agencies of local self-government.

Legislative assemblies do exist at the regional level but are entirely subordinate to the governors, if only because they are paid by the provinces' executive branches. (The election of governors is only a recent development and far from widespread; most governors were appointed by the president.)

There exists no legal framework or financial means for the creation of local self-government; people will have no choice but to achieve it through social struggle. All that really exists is the government hierarchy, from the president and national government on down.

That hierarchy is duplicated by a second, consisting of those appointed as the "President's representatives" (spies) in every region. The Constitution of 1993, which was passed hastily and not in a manner to inspire confidence, groans under the weight of the president's power. The rights it allocates to the state Duma are exceedingly constrained.

The 1996 Election

Given that structure of power, it is the presidential elections, held every four years, that are most important to the fate of the nation. But the 1996 election was not an occasion for serious deliberation, nor could it have been. A "communist cloud" hung over the elections—could the Communists really return to power?—and that hampered the voters. Mr. Yeltsin's side harped on that threat, presenting itself as the country's sole salvation. But even the Communists themselves were wary of coming to power, seeing no way out of the overall crisis.

The worst sorts of costly campaign spectacles were staged, at state expense, of course. Under such conditions, there were no campaign debates or speeches of substance. No one even discussed the candidates' programs.

Presented to the public only some ten days before the election, the published programs consisted of one hundred to two hundred pages of vague text. There was no time for the electorate to sit down and read the proposals, analyze them, and receive answers to their questions. Every last channel of the state-owned television network broadcast incessant barrages of propaganda favoring the incumbent head of state; there was no possibility of presenting opposing views.

After numerous invitations from the so-called independent television station, NTV, I agreed to a ten-minute interview in which I stated that both of the main contenders, the communist leader Gennadi A. Zyuganov and Mr. Yeltsin, were burdened with serious crimes against the interests of the people—

one for seventy long years, the other for five. I urged the electorate to vote against both, which would cause the elections to be postponed and allow new candidates to run. But NTV chopped my interview down to two ragged minutes, and my remarks were rendered incoherent and meaningless.

Tom Toles ©1993 Universal Press Syndicate. Reprinted with permission of Universal Press Syndicate. All rights reserved.

Thus did the president come to power a second time, without having been held responsible for all the defects of his previous term. This system of centralized power cannot be called a democracy.

Russia's Ruling Oligarchy

The rulers' important motives, decisions, intentions, and actions, as well as shifts in personnel, are completely opaque to society at large and come to light as only as faits accomplis. Shuffles in personnel are presented in formulations that say nothing: "according to a report submitted" and "in connection with a transfer to different work" (often not indicated). Even when a person is clearly culpable of some wrongdoing, there is no public explanation. The authorities operate on a moral imperative: We don't betray our own and we don't uncover their wrongdoing. So the fate of the country is now decided by a stable oligarchy of one-hundred-fifty to two hundred people, which includes the nimbler members of the old communist system's top and middle ranks, plus the nouveaux riches.

This is no tree of state grown up from roots but a dry stake driven into the ground or, as things now stand, an iron rod. The members of this oligarchy combine a lust for power with mercenary calculations. They exhibit no higher goals of serving the country and the people.

It could be said that throughout the last ten years of frenetic reorganization our government has not taken a single step unmarked by ineptitude. Worse, our ruling circles have not shown themselves in the least morally superior to the Communists who preceded them. Russia has been exhausted by crime, by the transfer into private hands of billions of dollars' worth of the nation's wealth. Not a single serious crime has been exposed, nor has there been a single public trial. The investigatory and judicial systems are severely limited in both their actions and their resources.

Meanwhile, since the Constitutional Court is a mere plaything and the state Duma only engages in the slackest of monitoring, a dozen "councils" (beginning with the notorious "Security Council") and "commissions" (with their instantly growing staffs) are forming around the president. The constitution does not provide for these bodies, which duplicate the work of the government and its ministerial branches, creating a system of irresponsible and chaotic multiple rule.

Was it so long ago that we thought there could exist no more absurd and unwieldy bureaucracy than that of the communist regime? But during the last ten years, the bureaucracy has doubled and tripled in size, all of it supported at the expense of a nation that is being reduced to beggary.

When a people is deprived of local self-government and when rights are neither guaranteed nor defended, those with the most initiative and talent can find few outlets for their creative powers, stonewalled by bureaucracy at every turn.

In what sort of democracy does a government calmly slumber while great numbers of people have not received their rightful salaries for half a year? Recently, in various places a new idea has emerged: "committees of salvation," meaning ad hoc local agencies, an alternative government that fights to keep the little that people have left in their ruined lives.

Unfair Elections

Most observers have come to recognize that Russia's elections have been largely free, but not at all fair. Incumbent officials at all levels mobilize the full force of the state to promote their candidacies through influence over the media, distribution of scarce resources to supporters or potential supporters, intimidation of challengers and outright fraud. While some elections probably are better than none, Russia's postindependence electoral history hardly justifies naming the country a democracy.

Paul J. Saunders, *Insight*, October 18, 1999.

In other countries, Russia's current situation would suffice for a major social explosion. But after seventy years of being bled white, after the selective annihilation of active, protesting elements, and now after a ten-year slide into mass destitution, Russia has no strength left for such an explosion, and there's none in the offing.

Russia's Economic Reforms

The so-called economic reforms—Mikhail Gorbachev's between 1987 and 1990, then Mr. Yeltsin's from 1992 to 1995—are another problem. Having noisily proclaimed the slogan of perestroika, Mr. Gorbachev was probably concerned with smoothly transferring party personnel into the new economic structure and safeguarding the party's own funds. He took no steps to create small- and middle-level private manufacturing, though he did wreck the system of vertical and horizontal links in the existing communist economy, which, though it worked badly, did work.

In that way, Mr. Gorbachev opened the door to economic chaos, a process further improved by Yegor T. Gaidar's "reform" and Anatoly B. Chubais's "privatization."

Genuine reform is a coordinated, systematic effort combining numerous measures aimed at a single goal. But from 1992 on, no such program was ever declared. Instead, there were two separate actions, which were not coordinated with each other, let alone with the economic benefit of the country.

One was Mr. Gaidar's "liberalizing of prices" in 1992. The lack of any competitive environment meant that monopolistic producers could inflate costs of production while at the same time reducing its volume and the outlays for it. This sort of "reform" quickly began to destroy production and, for much of the population, made consumer goods and many food items prohibitively expensive.

The other action was the frenzied privatization campaign. The campaign's first step was the government's issuing of vouchers to each citizen that supposedly represented his "share" of all the national wealth accumulated under the Communists. In reality, the total value of all the vouchers represented only a small fraction of 1 percent of that wealth.

The second step was the sell-off, not to say giveaway, of a multitude of state enterprises, including some gigantic ones. Those enterprises ended up in private hands, most of the new owners people seeking easy profit, with no experience of production and no desire to acquire any.

Organized Crime

Russia's economic chaos is made worse by organized crime, which, never nipped in the bud, is constantly stealing the country blind and accumulating enormous new capital. The gap between the rich and the impoverished majority has now assumed proportions unlike anything seen in the West or in prerevolutionary Russia. Each year, no less than $25 billion flows abroad into private accounts.

The destructive course of events over the last decade has come about because the government, while ineptly imitating foreign models, has completely disregarded the country's creativity and particular character as well as Russia's centuries-old spiritual and social traditions. Only if those paths are freed up can Russia be delivered from its near-fatal condition.

| "*Russia is by far the freest, most democratic nation of all the post-Soviet states save the three Baltic countries.*"

Russia Has Made Significant Progress in Achieving Democracy

Leon Aron

Many people have pronounced Russia a "failing state" in which democracy has failed to take hold and economic reforms have not brought prosperity. Because of this, writes Leon Aron in the following viewpoint, a debate has emerged within the United States over the question of "who lost Russia?" According to Aron, however, those who proclaim Russia to be "lost" fail to appreciate how far its political and economic conditions have improved since the waning days of the Soviet Union. Since 1991, he argues, Russia has held numerous contested elections on national and local levels, its press operates free of censorship, and political power has become more decentralized. Aron is director of Russian studies at the American Enterprise Institute and author of *Boris Yeltsin: A Revolutionary Life*.

As you read, consider the following questions:
1. What "myth" concerning Russia's 1996 presidential election does Aron seek to debunk?
2. What encouraging signs does the author perceive concerning Russia's 1998 financial crisis?
3. How does Aron respond to the charge that Russia is doomed by political and economic corruption?

S uddenly everyone is asking, Who lost Russia? . . .
Unfortunately, this important debate is being conducted like a kangaroo court. Not only have the accused—
both Americans and, especially, Russians—been tried and
found guilty in absentia, but, contrary to the Anglo-Saxon
legal tradition, the discovery stage, when the underlying
facts are established and each side presents its version of
events, has been skipped entirely. Before the sentence is
handed down, ought we not at least try to find out whether,
in fact, a crime has taken place: Has Russia, indeed, been
"lost" to the cause of the free market and democracy?

A hodgepodge of facts, half-truths, clichés, and distortions, the case for the prosecution comes down to a few simple postulates. First, free-market reforms have failed to make
Russia a prosperous country with a growing GDP. "Reform"
(a word rarely used without quotes these days) was nothing
but the "entrenchment of a kleptocracy in which corrupt officials ally with a few business magnates to send wealth out of
the country," according to Fritz Ermarth in the *New York
Times* of September 12 [1999]. "Reform" never enjoyed even
a modicum of popular support but was forced on a defenseless country by "reformers around Yeltsin" and their Western, especially International Monetary Fund, advisers with
the connivance of the White House. After eight years [since
1991], goes the indictment, Russia still does not have even an
approximation of a market economy. Instead, "reform" resulted in universal impoverishment. Today's Russia is a handful of thieving "oligarchs" feasting amidst the general penury.

In the political sphere, democratic institutions have not
taken root. This "Weimar Russia" is an unstable, "failing
state," in the words of [foreign policy expert] Condoleezza
Rice, . . . who has mentioned Russia in the same breath as
the "failed states" of North Korea and Iraq. As House [of
Representatives] majority leader Dick Armey so elegantly
put it, "Russia has become a looted and bankrupt zone of nuclearized anarchy."

In foreign policy, asserts the prosecution, [Russian presi-
dent] Boris Yeltsin has not delivered where America's core
national interests are concerned, and the "investment" in
him by the Clinton administration was wrong and a waste.

All these failures have soured the Russians on capitalism, democracy, the West in general, and the United States in particular and made them ripe for Communist *revanche*, anti-Western nationalist dictatorship, or an even scarier combination of the two.

Amnesia About Russia's Past

One of the most puzzling features of the argument that Russia has been "lost" is its ahistoricism. Post-Communist Russia is discussed as if it had no past. There seems to be total amnesia about the conditions that were so memorably exposed by *glasnost* in the waning years of the Soviet Union. For instance, in 1989, the last year of relative stability before the crisis became uncontrollable, the average salary in the Soviet Union was 200 rubles a month: $33 at the official exchange rate, $13 on the—still illegal—free currency market. (The average salary in Russia today [in 1999] is $75.) The Soviet Union was in 77th place in the world in personal consumption. Of 211 essential food products, only 23 were regularly available in state stores. Russians spent between 40 and 68 hours a month in queues. . . .

According to the minister of health, a total of 1,200,000 hospital beds (35 percent of the total) were in facilities with no hot water; every sixth hospital bed was in a facility with no running water at all; 30 percent of Soviet hospitals did not have indoor toilets. The Soviet Union had a higher rate of infant mortality than 49 nations, behind Barbados and the United Arab Emirates. Half of Soviet schools had no central heating, running water, or indoor toilets.

By the time Boris Yeltsin took over Russia in the fall of 1991, the country's economy was collapsing. Domestic production declined by 13 percent that year, the budget deficit soared to 30 percent of GDP, the annual inflation rate was 93 percent, hard currency and gold reserves were nearly exhausted, and the USSR defaulted on its international loans. No one who was in Moscow in the fall of 1991 will ever forget the absolutely bare shelves of the stores, the ration coupons for sugar, tobacco, and soap, and the sacks of potatoes stored on the balconies of apartment buildings in the center of Moscow, as their inhabitants prepared for famine.

Brief as it is, this sketch belies the postulate of a Russia "ruined" by reform. The picture we are offered of a handful of oligarchs presiding over a sea of starving millions is an equally crude caricature. Today the queues in stores—bane of four generations of Russians—have disappeared, and Russian shops, for the first time since the mid-1920s offer a cornucopia of quality food and goods. In 1997, for the first time in 40 years, Russia was self-sufficient in grain. In fact, it exported millions of tons of grain in 1998, even as agrobureaucrats in the Kremlin and the U.S. Department of Agriculture were arranging shipments from the United States to meet a nonexistent emergency.

While it is true that millions of people—especially retirees, collective farmers, and workers in the mammoth military-industrial complex—were impoverished by galloping inflation and cuts in state spending, millions more—urban, younger, and better educated (who voted for Yeltsin in overwhelming numbers in the 1996 presidential election)—saw a dramatic improvement in their professional and personal lives. For the first time in Russian history, there is a sizable middle class and intelligentsia outside state employ. . . .

The new Russian middle class suffered greatly in the [monetary] crisis of 1998, and it may take a few years for the standard of living to return to pre-crash levels. Yet there is no reason to doubt that this will happen. It may currently be all the rage in Washington to speak of Russia's "virtual economy," but we are suddenly discovering that a Russian market economy does exist after all and, despite its deep distortions, responds to economic stimuli much as any market economy would. In full accordance with supply-side theory, the continuing absence of price controls, a cheaper but stable national currency, and a drastic reduction of imports have unleashed domestic production. Russian-made food and goods fill the stores. Industrial production (or rather its registered and taxable part) was 4.5 percent higher in the first six months of 1999 than in the first six months of 1998, and it grew even faster after that. Contrary to many a forecast, there is no starvation. . . .

Another mainstay of the thesis that Russia has been "lost" is the claim that the Russians have rejected capitalism. In fact, after three generations entirely in state employ, Russians remain sharply divided on the issue of private vs. state ownership of the economy. In a national poll commissioned by the United States Information Agency at the beginning of 1999, 41 percent favored a "mostly" or "completely" state-owned economy, while 50 percent felt either that the economy should be "mostly" or "completely" privately owned (16 percent) or that it should be a "mix" of private and state ownership (34 percent).

In the 1995 Duma [Russian legislature] elections, 21 million votes (30 percent of the total) were cast for pro-reform and pro-government right-of-center parties, while the Communists and their allies received 22 million votes (32 percent). (Because of the splintering of the right-of-center parties, only Yabloko and Our Home is Russia crossed the 5 percent threshold required for Duma membership. A full 9.6 million votes cast for small right-of-center, pro-reform, and pro-government parties were wasted, and the Communists ended up with 35 percent more deputies than the right: 187 seats vs. 121 seats.)

The 1996 Election

Then there is the myth that Yeltsin won the 1996 presidential election by buying 40 million votes with the oligarchs' money. In reality, Russian voters that year made a monumental and informed choice worthy of a great people—a choice between two fundamentally different visions of Russia. Yeltsin ran on a platform of continuing but "modified" and "socially oriented" reforms, while Gennady Zyuganov, the Communist candidate, called for a return to state control (if not outright ownership) of the economy. Zyuganov presented his case to the public in a vigorous national campaign. Between January and July, the Communist alternative was expounded by over 150 pro-Communist local and national newspapers and magazines, the national dailies alone with a combined circulation of over 10 million. Tens of thousands of Communist organizers campaigned door to door. Millions of leaflets were distributed. And the Communists enjoyed three and a half hours of free prime time on national television and held hundreds of campaign rallies.

Although most Russians tell pollsters they are dissatisfied with the "way democracy works" in their country, solid majorities reject a restoration of "order" if the price is forgoing key civil and political liberties—habeas corpus limits on police, the freedom to hold political meetings and demonstrations, free elections, the right to travel abroad, and an uncensored press. In 1994 virtually equal proportions of respondents supported and opposed a dictatorship to "restore order in Russia" (35 percent and 33 percent respectively). In 1997, the opposition to a dictatorship grew to 55 percent, while support stagnated at 35 percent.

Allegedly a "failing" state and "zone of nuclearized anarchy," Russia in the past six years has held three free national elections (two parliamentary and one presidential), two national referenda, and in each of its 89 provinces at least one (sometimes two) election for a legislature and governor. On only one occasion—the Duma elections and simultaneous constitutional referendum in December 1993, three months after the bloodshed at Russia's parliament building—did turnout fall below 64 percent of eligible voters. Nearly 70 million Russians (just under 70 percent of all eligible adults) voted in the presidential election in 1996. There were 50 human rights groups in Russia in 1996. Today, there are 1,200.

New Freedoms

This is a regime that—even with its many very real, even gross flaws—is the most open and liberal in the country's history. The press is free from government censorship. The opposition, no matter how radical, can publish and campaign for office. Free and fiercely competitive multi-candidate elections are the norm at both the local and national levels. After a thousand years of authoritarianism and totalitarianism, Russia is radically decentralized, yet whole, with political power dispersed both geographically among the regions and among diverse centers of power on the national level. No party (much less person, even the president) can dominate and mold Russian national politics at will.

Following the Constitutional Court's lead, local judges routinely rule against local government agencies (as when the latter tried to restrict the activities of "foreign" religious denominations), the Kremlin, the army (when it sought to punish conscientious objectors), and the secret police (as in the espionage cases of Captain Grigoriy Pas'ko in the Far East and Captain Alexander Nikitin in St. Petersburg). In a typical instance of citizens' taking on the government in court, last July [1999] an Internet provider in the southern city of Volgograd rejected the demand of the Federal Security Service that the company monitor its customers' use of the Web. The security agency retaliated by blocking the firm's use of the satellite channel that gave it access to the Web. The firm brought suit against the FSB, and a decision is pending [as of October 1999].

Democratic Habits in Russia

Fortunately, democratic habits are among the world's most benign addictions, and are starting to spread in Russia.

It is easy to forget that a decade ago [in 1989], the Communist party was still the only one allowed by the constitution. Today, there is a whole lot of democracy going on.

Russians enjoy greater liberties than at any time in history. The press is outspoken and varied. Civil society is expanding rapidly. And Russians have grown accustomed to voting regularly and speaking their minds freely.

Address by Madeleine K. Albright before the Carnegie Endowment for International Peace, September 16, 1999.

Although woefully inadequate by the standards of older democracies, Russia is by far the freest, most democratic nation of all the post-Soviet states save the three Baltic countries. Even as severe a test as the past year's financial crisis [in 1998], with the devaluation of the ruble and the government's default on its domestic debt, did not result in riots and the disintegration of authority, as in Indonesia, or in show trials of high-level scapegoats and the jailing of journalists, as in Malaysia. There was not the slightest infringement of human rights or political liberties, curtailment of the press, or harassment of the opposition. The Communists' attempt to capitalize on the crisis failed miserably when the much ballyhooed "Red October" turned out at best 200,000 people on the streets—in a country of 150 million. . . .

The Problem of Corruption

By far the most solid charge brought against Russia by the doomsayers is corruption. This scourge saps the legitimacy of the state, distorts the market, impedes foreign investment, and ultimately costs Russian consumers and taxpayers trillions of rubles every year. Before it was suddenly discovered by the "Who lost Russia?" crew, the subject had been discussed by scholars for years. The problem here is not that the critics have the facts wrong (although they indulge in hyperbole), but that they fail to locate this evil in its historic and geographic context.

Inconvenient though it may be to American columnists and members of Congress, the truth is that Northwest European-style capitalism—originally Protestant, Anglo-Saxon and Scandinavian—is very rare in the world today. Most countries will require decades, perhaps centuries, of experience with the free market and democracy before they attain a similar standard. The going is likely to be especially rough in Russia's neighborhood—which, from Romania and Bulgaria to Turkey, Iran, Iraq, Afghanistan, Pakistan, and China, has been notoriously corrupt for centuries. . . .

Like its neighbors, Russia has been corrupt for centuries. But corruption reached its apogee under the Communists. By extirpating, suppressing, or subverting the civil and governmental institutions that promote self-restraint and personal responsibility (the church, charities, professional associations, and an independent judiciary), by censoring everything that was published, by making the party *nomenklatura* immune from criminal prosecution, Soviet totalitarianism achieved universal thievery and bribery. . . .

The burden of this history is compounded by the realities of economic transition. In the no-man's-land between the state-controlled economy and the free market—where some restrictions have been removed while others remain, and former state property is left defenseless as a beached whale—the hungry, newly empowered entrepreneur meets the impoverished bureaucrat or politician, who sells him access to the beach. Corruption of this type was or is a problem in Carlos Menem's Argentina, Fernando Cordoso's Brazil, Carlos Salinas's Mexico, Kim Dae Jung's South Korea, Turgut

Ozal's Turkey, Nelson Mandela's South Africa, and all the post-Communist nations without exception. (Russia, indeed, is the least corrupt of the countries of the former USSR, with the exception of the Baltics.) . . .

Of course, neither history nor political culture absolves the guilty. They do, however, have clear policy implications. The roots of Russian corruption go much deeper than the alleged mistakes and personal frailties of Yeltsin and the "reformers." In societies where corruption is hereditary, the problem can be alleviated only by decades of democratic politics and press freedom, over several post-Communist generations. In the meantime, we ought to be realistic, patient, and firm in our rejection of sanctions against corrupt practices and officials. . . .

It would be a terrible blunder to make Russian corruption synonymous with the failure of Russia's grand experiment in free-market economics. There is a critical distinction between the countries where corruption overwhelms the state and the economy and leads to a breakdown or permanent crisis (Albania, Indonesia, Venezuela, Colombia) and those where corruption, no matter how ubiquitous, still allows for democratic order, economic progress, and integration in the world economy (Italy, Turkey). Russia appears to be evolving along the latter path.

The Problem of "Presentism"

In his book *Abraham Lincoln and the Second American Revolution*, James McPherson, refuting revisionist historians' claim that the Civil War and Reconstruction accomplished little, charged his opponents with "presentism," a tendency to "read history backwards, measuring change over time from the point of arrival rather than the point of departure." McPherson compared this mode of observation to "looking through the wrong end of a telescope—everything appears smaller than it really is."

A similar distortion underlies the myth that Russia is "lost." Post-Communist Russia's epic experiment with self-rule, political liberty, and the free market is like the progress of a long and disorderly wagon train trekking across a vast and swampy plane, stopping, zigzagging, occasionally almost drowning in mud, yet stubbornly plowing forward. Following close behind but never quite catching up with the caravan is a crowd of journalists and experts. Their heads are hanging. They look neither forward, to see where the road might lead; nor back, to measure the astonishing distance already covered; nor even to the sides, to compare the caravan's progress with that of Russia's neighbors. They look only downward, at the dirt on the wheels, the ruts in the road, and the ugly swamp creatures awakened by the wagon train's passage and feasting on the refuse in its wake.

A longer and broader view yields different observations. There is a great deal in today's Russia that, to the citizen of a mature liberal democracy, appears flawed or even appalling. Yet measured from "the point of departure," the progress is undeniable and enormous.

"Russians today simply lack that sense of civic responsibility that underlies the proper functioning of democratic institutions in the West."

Russia's History and Culture Preclude the Creation of a Democratic Society

W. Bruce Lincoln

In the following viewpoint, W. Bruce Lincoln, a history professor at Northern Illinois University, contends that Russia has a strong historical legacy of autocracy that goes back centuries. Because of this tradition of rule imposed from above—a tradition enshrined by decades of Communist rule—the Russian people lack the sense of civic responsibility that enables democracies to function in other countries. Lincoln predicts that at some point in the future, Russians will probably look to a dictatorial leader to establish internal order and reclaim Russia's place as a world power.

As you read, consider the following questions:

1. What has been the consistent result in Russia's history when its rulers have attempted to open public debate about national goals, according to Lincoln?
2. What impact did the Bolshevik Revolution have on Russia's political development, in Lincoln's view?
3. What is the source of national pride in Russia, according to the author?

Reprinted from W. Bruce Lincoln, "Why Democracy Won't Work in Russia," *Chronicles: A Magazine of American Culture*, October 1999. This magazine is a publication of The Rockford Institute, 928 N. Main St., Rockford, IL 61103; www.chroniclesmagazine.org. Reprinted with permission from the publisher.

Russia is in crisis again. Bad debts, devalued currency, corrupt officials, a political system that verges on paralysis, competing visions of the future that allow no room for compromise—the list of problems grows longer as its components become more complex.

Observers attribute the crisis to the huge difficulties connected with trying to transform a once-inert socialist economy into a dynamic capitalist one. They see the crushing weight of Russia's Soviet heritage as the evil force underlying these problems. And they hope for a knight in shining armor to save Mother Russia in her hour of need.

Russia's Anti-Democratic Heritage

Hopeful Western observers (and not a few opportunistic Russians courting Western support) insist that the knight will wear the mantle of Western-style democracy. But the facts of Russian history argue otherwise. Not only has Russia not tried democracy until now, but its history shows that its leaders have always attempted to solve its many crises by anti-democratic means.

The currents of Russia's anti-democratic heritage run broad and deep. More than 70 years of Soviet life instilled attitudes that worked against democratic institutions. And, except for a few decades before the Revolution of 1917, Russia's historical experience under the Romanovs [Russia's ruling dynasty from 1613 to 1917] followed the same course. Russia's historical legacy calls upon its leaders to command and its people to obey. Taking responsibility for their nation's destiny is not something that ordinary Russians have done in the past. Nor do they seem ready to do so now.

Whether Romanov or Soviet, Russia's heritage is autocratic. Reform in Russia has always come from above, from a czar or commissar who has imposed change upon a nation of self-serving interest groups that have been unwilling to think in terms of national interest. Russia's masses have not been accustomed to serving their nation. They have instead served rulers who have imposed national service upon them.

In the past, national interest has been a matter for Russia's rulers to define. And progress toward national goals has usually come when those rulers decided that the nation's interests required change. This was true of Peter the Great and Alexander II (who freed 45 million serfs and state peasants from bondage in the 1860's). It was also true of [Vladimir I.] Lenin and [Joseph] Stalin, and more recently [Mikhail] Gorbachev.

Difficulties with *Glasnost*

The belief that reform must be imposed from above has made Russia's rulers jealous of their power. That principle has lain at the heart of their policies, and it has stood in the way of every effort to draw the Russians more directly into public life. Open participation in civic affairs—what the Russians nowadays call *glasnost*—has been tried only rarely in the past, and almost always with unfortunate results.

Whenever Russia's rulers have tried to open public debate about their nation's course, they have inevitably confronted the dilemma posed by popular expectations that rise more quickly than their ability (or willingness) to meet them. Catherine the Great initiated a public debate on Russia's relationship to the West in the 1760's, but she had to end her experiment when attention shifted from the issues of culture and enlightenment to the problems posed by serfdom and the arbitrary authority it encouraged.

Alexander II tried *glasnost* at the beginning of the Great Reform era in the 1860's, only to to be obliged to cut the debate short when it began to question the viability of autocracy itself. And a century and a quarter later, Gorbachev saw his effort to open public debate about the shortcomings of communism destroy the Soviet Union in the space of six short years.

Difficulties with *glasnost* in the past have shown Russia's rulers that any public participation in government can threaten their ability to impose change from above. And the fact that the Russians have historically been either too divided or self-interested to think in terms of their nation's best interests has made rulers hesitant to relinquish their power to impose change. Too often, the alternative to a strong and determined ruler has been a society fragmented to the point where all sense of national interest has been lost. We are seeing that today, in the conflicts within the

Duma [Russian parliament] and the tensions between the Duma and [President Boris] Yeltsin's government.

Russians Lack Civic Responsibility

Russians today simply lack that sense of civic responsibility that underlies the proper functioning of democratic institutions in the West. Men and women made cynical by the blatant abuses of power they witnessed during the Soviet era do not understand that, in a democratic society, citizens are expected to take responsibility for the well-being of their communities and their neighbors. Most of all, citizens in a democracy must take responsibility for themselves, but there is no deep-rooted sense among present-day Russians that requires them to think of their nation's welfare, pay their taxes, and discharge their justly-contracted debts.

Yeltsin's government (as Russian governments have done for hundreds of years) continues to exploit its citizens by devaluing the currency and defaulting on loans. Its citizens continue to respond by evading taxes and embezzling government funds. Russia's leaders do not understand that a government has to be based on promises made and promises kept. Nor do citizens understand that democracy requires them to honor and serve any government the people elect to represent them.

Although Russians have traditionally been willing to bow to their rulers' authority, there was a brief time when a broadly based sense of civic responsibility seemed about to take root. The Great Reforms of the 1860's and 1870's not only freed millions of serfs, but also created new institutions of local self-government, a modern judicial system, and a citizen army. These required the Russians to take responsibility for themselves, their communities, and the defense of their country as citizens are supposed to do. Such changes did not come overnight, but by the end of the 19th century, they had taken firm root.

For a time at the beginning of this century, this growing sense of civic responsibility led Russia's citizens to seek a voice in determining their nation's destiny. Some believed that czar and people should unite in a monarchical or democratic polity. Others shared a more revolutionary vision, in which the will of the people alone could determine Russia's course. And both groups looked toward a future in which the voices of citizens would be heard. Both argued that making one's voice heard was a citizen's duty.

The Communists Take Power

In 1917, conflicts between these two visions of Russia's future led to a revolution that destroyed the sense of civic responsibility that had begun to take shape. Lenin and his triumphant Bolsheviks shaped Russia's political values around party loyalty and party discipline, not the civic virtues that encouraged independent thought and dissent. Many of the men and women whose call for civic responsibility had played a part in bringing on the Revolution fled abroad. Those who remained in Russia disappeared into execution chambers and forced labor camps.

By the time Stalin seized power in 1928, all vestiges of an independent citizenry had been swept from Russia. Because there was no place in a society governed by party discipline for the sort of civic responsibility that could lead to disagreement or dissent, the all-powerful Soviet state took charge of its citizens' welfare. In the long term, this may have been the most corrosive of all the legacies that the Soviet experience bequeathed.

In return for guaranteeing the minimum of human needs and social benefits required for survival, the Soviet state deprived its citizens of any power to shape their lives. Russians had to pay lip service to the principles that would best enable them to get ahead in a world in which the state held command of life's luxuries and necessities.

In Soviet times, the state spoke in the name of the people, while each person sought to wrest whatever he could from the state. State propaganda applauded the people's participation in state-controlled civic life, but in reality it was every person for himself, with each trying to serve as many narrow personal interests as possible. It became every citizen's task to negotiate directly with the state for the small perquisites that could make life better.

A better apartment, a free vacation, tickets to the opera, and access to special stores became each person's urgent concerns. For what separated poverty from luxury in Soviet Russia was neither wealth nor talent, but the favor of the state. That favor could be purchased only by loyalty, and expressions of that loyalty were expected at every level of human endeavor. In such a society, the possibilities for corruption were endless. The moral imperatives that go hand-in-hand with civic responsibility in democratic societies simply had no place or meaning in Russia after 1928.

Democracy Has Not Taken Root

We should not assume that democracy has taken root in Russia. Most Russians, frankly, consider their rulers corrupt and criminal. Just because they were elected through a democratic process does not mean that they have legitimacy in the eyes of most Russians. Democracy rests on thin ice in Russia, and facing further economic turmoil will only strain Russia's embryonic democratic institutions like never before. The fact is that the risk of a return to a dictatorship of some kind in Russia is higher than at any time since the fall of the Soviet Union. We should stop thinking in black-white contrasts of what existed before and what must exist in the future.

Kim R. Holmes, *Heritage Lectures*, no. 629, January 8, 1999.

Whether looked at from the perspective of decades or centuries, such historical experiences are not the material from which democratic societies are easily fashioned. The hard truth may be that Russia's is not the sort of experience from which democracy can be forged at all. For centuries, reform, progress, change, law and order, the definition of national priorities and interests, and the visions of where Russia needs to go and what its future ought to be all have been handed down from above. It is small wonder, then, that the Russians are carrying little sense of civic responsibility with them as they approach the 21st century. The belief that one must answer for oneself and one's community cannot be legislated into being, nor is it one of those self-evident truths that are destined to be eagerly seized upon whenever the forces of history make it available.

Few people would deny that a great deal of Western money is stolen by Russian officials, bankers, and businessmen. Money from the West simply creates more opportunities for the sorts of corruption in which Russians have engaged for centuries. "We all steal," one of Peter the Great's closest advisers remarked at the beginning of the 18th century. "The only difference is that some of us do it on a larger and more conspicuous scale." Bolstered by the eradication of civic responsibility that the Soviet experience demanded, that statement is more true today than ever before.

National Pride

Although it has deprived them of those values and experiences that lie at the heart of the successful workings of democracy, history has given the Russians a powerful sense of national pride. At different times, Russia has claimed to be the last refuge of true Christianity and the forerunner of the new communist world order. It helped to rid Europe of the tyranny of Napoleon, played a key part in the destruction of Nazi Germany, and reigned as one of the world's two superpowers for more than 40 years.

Of these claims and accomplishments, the Russians are intensely—and justifiably—proud. Being reduced to the status of poor cousins in the community of great powers is not something that they can accept with good grace. If the experiment with democracy fails to restore the Russians to the place in world affairs that they consider to be rightfully theirs, then one can expect to see leaders and people embrace those principles that have served them so well in the past. In that case, they will turn sharply away from democracy and re-establish those regimes that marshaled the nation's human, political, and economic resources with so much success in days gone by. The impact of such a turn is difficult to calculate. But it certainly will take Russia in a very different direction from the one that Western leaders want it to follow.

"Today,…[Russia] is in the midst of a democratic revolution."

Russia Has Overcome Its Authoritarian Heritage to Create a Democratic Revolution

Alexander Elder

Alexander Elder, a native of Leningrad who was raised in Estonia, was a ship's doctor when he defected from the Soviet Union in 1973 and received political asylum in the United States. He has since worked as a psychiatrist and financial trader and has traveled extensively throughout the former Soviet Union since its 1991 demise. The following viewpoint is excerpted from his book *From Rubles to Dollars*, a guide to investing in Russia. Elder argues that Russians have succeeded remarkably in reversing a centuries-old tradition of autocratic rule. He describes the political upheavals Russia experienced in the 1990s and contends that Russia is a much freer and more open society compared with the totalitarian Soviet regime. Fears that Russia will revert to a dictatorship are unfounded, he concludes, because most Russian people are united in their support for democracy.

As you read, consider the following questions:
1. How did the government of the Soviet Union repress its people, according to Elder?
2. How have Russians been affected by the attempted coups of 1991 and 1993, according to the author?

Excerpted from Alexander Elder, *From Rubles to Dollars: Making Money on Russia's Exploding Financial Frontier*. Reprinted with permission from the New York Institute of Finance.

Even a brief look at Russia's history reveals centuries of brutal oppression. Today, the nation that succeeded in liberating itself is in the midst of a democratic revolution.

More than six centuries ago the nomad hordes of Ghengis Khan erupted from the steppes (prairies) of Mongolia, riding west for thousands of miles. They burned, looted, raped, and killed until they came to a halt in what is now Austria. Their devastating and murderous sweep across Russia was followed by two hundred years of brutal occupation. . . .

The Mongol occupation collapsed after two centuries, although their raids continued for another century. The Russian nobles and bishops remembered all too well the horrible price they had paid for their disjointed and ineffective defense. They wanted a strong central power, and for the next 300 years Russia was saddled with one of the most repressive dynasties in Europe.

The tsar of a hundred million people rode the streets of his capital in a carriage looking for nobles who might be smoking in public. (Sniffing tobacco was considered a healthy Russian habit, while smoking was a noxious foreign influence.) While Western Europe was booming with the Industrial Age, most Russians still lived as serfs (indentured peasants) in remote villages, whipped at will by their masters. The tiny ruling elite found it easy to extract enough wealth from the huge country, so they had no interest in developing its economy. There was no middle class to speak of—just masses of serfs and a small landed aristocracy. The tsars repressed, exiled, or chased out of the country many of its best creative minds, especially writers—Pushkin, Lermontov, Dostoyevsky, Turgenev. Amazingly, in that repressive atmosphere, Russia developed and sustained one of the most vibrant cultures anywhere in the world. . . .

In 1918, the last members of the hapless Romanov dynasty ended their lives at the bottom of a Siberian mine shaft with bullet holes in their skulls. The murder of any individual is a tragedy, but recent attempts by Russian monarchists to elevate the last tsar to the status of a saint ignore the fact that his ineptitude helped bring the Bolshevik cruelty not just upon the royal family, but upon the entire nation. . . .

The communists who overthrew the tsar made him look

like an amateur in the business of repression. Where a tsar hung five military officers for demonstrating against him, Trotsky and Lenin put thousands of officers, guilty only of having served in the tsar's army, into barges, towed them offshore, and sank them. Where the tsars hanged revolutionary gunrunners off telegraph poles, the communists hanged thousands of men and women in villages and towns that dared to resist their rule.

Six centuries of brutal repression did not break the Russian spirit. After two centuries of Mongol rule, three centuries of a repressive monarchy, and nearly a century of bloodthirsty communists, long-suffering Russia was liberated in 1991. It was an almost bloodless revolution. The old system crumbled after the government could no longer hold the empire together. There had been no general uprising, simply the falling apart of the old, and a spontaneous emergence of a democracy. Russia had freed itself not just from communism—it liberated itself from six centuries of repression. Since then, would-be strongmen tried to roll back the clock twice—and the nation rose to resist them and kept its freedom.

Profound Change

Casual visitors cannot comprehend the depth and speed of changes in Russia in recent years. Even locals, caught in their daily grind, often lose sight of the fantastic changes in their country.

Visitors see Coca-Cola signs, people in jeans, *The Wall Street Journal* on newsstands, and a chain of religious stores owned by the Moscow Patriarchy. It seems like a pretty normal landscape, with some local color.

These and other seemingly casual signs reflect profound political, social, and economic changes. The Soviet empire fiercely fought change; it jailed, exiled, and killed its opponents. The Soviet Union was a repressive behemoth whose ham-fisted control of its people grew like a cancer, metastasizing at a crazy speed, following a sick logic of its own. It began at birth—the state laid down the rules for a family's first contact with its newborn. It continued after death—if a family dared to arrange a religious funeral, the state punished the survivors. . . .

A child old enough to go to school would come for the first time into the field of vision of the KGB, the dreaded secret police. Private schools were outlawed, and public schools promoted the cult of Pavlik Morozov. When city communists came to his village to confiscate grain in the 1920s, Pavlik showed them where his parents hid theirs. They were arrested and exiled to Siberia, and Pavlik's uncle slit the boy's throat. The Soviet propaganda machine sanctified the informer boy.

I was six years old when my parents and grandparents began to warn me, "Do not tell anyone what you hear at home." They listened to the Voice of America behind closed doors and drawn curtains, spoke highly of the West, and laughed at the government, but both my parents were communist party members. At their jobs, they sat at party meetings and raised their hands in approval of party resolutions. Several generations of Soviet children grew up like that, learning to hide and lay low. No wonder so many Soviets grew up stiff and suspicious. . . .

Soviet Oppression

Out on the streets of the Soviet Union, groups of *druzhinniki*, (police auxiliaries), harassed people whose clothes were politically incorrect. They could catch a *stilyaga* (sharp dresser) and cut open his tight pant legs, or mess up a tall hairdo on a girl, or break her spike heels. . . .

It was a crime to be in business or even to be self-employed. An elderly neighbor who helped my parents buy a good winter coat and two spare tires had been arrested, convicted of being a *makler* (broker) and sent to a labor camp for two years. The government had the monopoly on the means of production. Underground businessmen could make astronomic profits, but had to hide. Every entrepreneur was a criminal by definition because he used equipment that belonged to the state. All businessmen risked their freedom, but the reward for the most successful was death. If you made a million and the government caught you, it called that "an extra large theft of state property," and could shoot you after a show trial. . . .

Each citizen above the age of 16 had to carry an "internal passport" stamped with his or her address. It was a crime to live away from one's assigned place for more than three days without registering with the police. The law was rarely enforced against vacationers or tourists, but often used to harass dissidents and keep peasants down on collective farms.

The "Iron Curtain" that surrounded the USSR not only limited foreigners' access to the country, it imprisoned Soviet citizens. The entire country was ringed with barbed wire, tripwires, and a 6-meter (18 ft.) wide strip of specially smoothed dirt to detect the tracks of would-be escapees. No wonder political prisoners called labor camps "the small zone" and the country "the big zone." Half a million guards patrolled the border with dogs, searchlights, and helicopters. Running away was a capital offense, but desperate men, such as myself, kept taking chances. . . .

Millions had been killed during the 74-year war the Soviet government waged against its own people. Entire layers of society had been summarily sentenced to death and imprisonment—tsarist military officers, priests, aristocrats, Cossacks, successful peasants, political dissidents. They were shot, or hanged, or died a slow death in labor camps.

The Communist Collapse

The Communist Party and the KGB held the Soviet Empire by its gills, while a huge army protected it from any external threat. The system had been built to last and even to try to conquer the world. The ship of the state sank after its captain cracked open the door to reform—and the flood of change rushed in.

Mikhail Gorbachev, who came into power in 1985, was the last communist tsar. He may have been more inclined to liberalize the system because his and his wife's families had been victimized during the Stalin era. In trying to revive the stagnant Soviet economy, Gorbachev introduced two new concepts—*glasnost* and *perestroika*. *Glasnost* (literally, "voiceness") meant speaking up and criticizing mistakes. This may sound normal to a Westerner, but it was a revolutionary concept in the USSR, where many generations had been brutally subdued into silence. *Perestroika* (literally, rebuilding) permitted a small degree of private enterprise.

Once the people could speak with impunity, the shouts

suppressed for over 70 years broke from their throats. Once they got a chance to run their own businesses, they started abandoning their state jobs. The old system could not take the stress of change and began to crumble. Gorbachev, who remained a card-carrying communist, had nothing against the Soviet system. He was its product and its beneficiary and only tried to improve it. He was flabbergasted when, in response to his reforms, the Soviet system began falling apart.

Lurie's World ©1992 Worldwide Copyright by Cartoonews International Syndicate, NYC, USA. Reprinted with permission.

Magazines and newspapers started publishing political exposés. The mass murders of political opponents, . . . the century-long history of communist lies, repression, and exploitation were opened up to the public. At first, many journalists feared arrest, but when nobody came after them, the media grew bold and its revelations helped wash away the last remaining shreds of the system's legitimacy. The communists were like Dracula—both drank blood in the dark and could not survive the light of day.

Private businesses began to open up in the late 1980s. Their right to exist was still uncertain—the laws against them were still on the books. A vice-president of the Russian Exchange said to me lightheartedly in April 1997, while we were waiting for the annual meeting to begin, "For the first four years we all worked under the article of the Criminal Code—ten years imprisonment with confiscation of property."

As the dam of prohibitions erected over 74 years began to crumble, new opportunities came in like a flood. Interest rates rocketed above 100%, but businesses could earn 100% in three months. The impregnable Iron Curtain became more like Swiss cheese. Imports and exports soared, nobody paid any taxes, the government treasury was emptied. Without subsidies, inefficient state industries started grinding to a halt.

Democrats and nationalists in Eastern Europe began to stir. The communist regimes of Czechoslovakia and Poland imploded and fell. Germany became reunited just months after the last two men had been shot trying to scale the Berlin Wall. The earlier Soviet rulers would have ruthlessly repressed their satellites, but Gorbachev's government lost its sense of purpose. The military literally ran out of gas. The men in the Kremlin stared in a groggy stupor at the changes they had unleashed, but could no longer control.

The 1991 Coup

As the empire started to disintegrate, the increasingly restive Soviet parliament had scheduled a crucial vote. No longer a rubber stamp for the Central Committee of the Communist Party, it was going to vote whether to maintain the Soviet Union or let its restive members go. The Communist Party of the Soviet Union had a century-long history of armed intervention on the eve of important votes. On the eve of the 1991 vote, a group of old communist bosses staged a coup, trying to turn back the tide.

In August 1991, while Gorbachev was vacationing at a Black Sea *dacha* (summer house), they seized control of the central government. The *putchists*, as the plotters came to be called, hoped to swing Gorbachev to their side, but, just in case they could not, they put him and his family under house arrest. The *putchists* had been just as incompetent running a coup as they had been running the country in their earlier days. The first thing they did after announcing their takeover on TV was to have a party and drink themselves into a stupor. They never secured the Moscow TV tower, its City Hall, or most other potential resistance centers. Boris Yeltsin, the firebrand president of the Russian Republic, the largest component of the Soviet Union, fired by Gorbachev from the central government just a year earlier, rapidly emerged as the leader of the democratic resistance.

Yeltsin had been away from Moscow on the day of the coup. With great personal courage, he flew back into Moscow to organize resistance. He managed to land and get into his office because the incompetent plotters had forgotten to seal the airports.

Yeltsin rallied the democrats from his office in the Russian White House, ringed by a thin line of loyal police and armed guards sent by private security agencies. An American hotel owner loaned Yeltsin his cell phone, allowing him to keep in touch with the media even after his phone lines had been cut. Volunteers streamed to the White House and built barricades against the assault—but it never came. The plotters, bruised by fierce public resistance turned to the military; but the Russian army has no tradition of coups. When the army refused to join the fight, the rebellion collapsed.

Three persons were killed in the coup. The *putchists* were released after a few years in jail and an unsuccessful prosecution. There was an emotional backlash against the communists, and their party was briefly outlawed. Gorbachev was widely perceived as having lost control and prestige. Yeltsin met with the presidents of Ukraine and Belarus, the two largest Slavic republics. The three had agreed to separate, effectively ending the existence of the Soviet Union. Gorbachev, the president of the USSR, no longer had a country—and Yeltsin, who had publicly resigned from the Communist Party, remained president of the largest, richest, and most powerful component of the old Soviet empire. . . .

The 1993 Crisis

Two years later Russia was in for another communist coup attempt. In 1993 Boris Yeltsin came to loggerheads with the *Duma* (the Russian parliament). Its communist deputies were blocking his reforms and trying to roll them back. Yeltsin publicly questioned the legitimacy of those deputies, since half of them had been appointed under the old regime rather than elected.

Russia's new constitution was still too raw and did not have a clear mechanism for resolving such conflicts between the branches of government (it now does). Yeltsin was prepared to wait for the next election, but the communist members of *Duma* had other plans. They stockpiled weapons in the Parliament building and called on their supporters to come join them. Moscow communists rushed to the Duma and attacked the TV center in Ostankino on the outskirts of Moscow. The city saw another night of skirmishes: firefights between rebels and the city police, crowds of democracy supporters rallying to build barricades and protect the Ostankino TV tower.

The old communists' planning had been slipshod and inefficient as usual. They counted on the support of the army whose officer corps was heavily communist—but the army remained in its barracks. Yeltsin ordered a tank unit from the elite Kantemirov Guards division into the city. The tanks circled the *Duma* building in the center of Moscow, gave its defenders an ultimatum, and opened fire. The rebels surrendered, their leaders were arrested, but released after two years without a trial. In 1996 Alexander Rutskoi, one of the coup leaders, won a democratic gubernatorial election in the Kursk region, southwest of Moscow, in the heart of Russia.

Speaking of beating back the coup, there are several thousand persons in Moscow who recognize one another from the barricades of 1991 and 1993. They risked their lives and the future of their families to protect the fledgling democracy and fight communism—and won. Victory was far from certain in those days, and a strong sense of camaraderie persists. I have noticed in recent years that more and more people speak of having been there (the barricades are becoming more crowded with the passage of time). It reminds me of Americans claiming descent from the Mayflower, which has been called "the largest ship in history."

In 1996, Russia held its first democratic presidential election—a watershed event in the nation's history. The establishment threw its support to Yeltsin, who won with 52% of the popular vote, against 40% for Zyuganov, the communist candidate. Communists hinted darkly at a social disorder if they lost the election, but in the end were remarkably gracious in their defeat.

Will They Return?

Many casual observers in the US, Australia, Europe, and Asia have said to me they feared that Russia's anticommunist revolution of 1991 will become undone. They think a new strongman may emerge, grab power, roll back the clock and return us all to the days of living under the threat of Russian intercontinental ballistic missiles.

These are empty fears.

Russian reforms are irreversible—the country will not tolerate a new strongman. As the waves of democratic elections roll across the land, people keep voting time and again for democracy and capitalism. The communist opposition is splintered, broke, devoid of ideas, and has lost its access to the mass media. The majority, not only the elite, are benefiting from the reforms. The Russian army never staged a coup, and its military machine is a broken, rusting hulk.

The Russian army is in a sad state today, hungry and demoralized. It lost the [1994–1996] war in Chechnya, its officers are selling blood to help feed their families, and suicide is the largest cause of death among the military. . . .

On May 9, 1997, Victory Day, an emotional public holiday in the country that had lost 19 million people in World War II, the army did not have enough money for its customary parade of military hardware in Red Square. They could afford only a 50-minute march by several units, representing different services. The fatal weakness of the military machine is good for the young democracy.

Free, vigorously contested elections are taking place all over the vast expanse of Russia. Not just Presidential elections, but many local ones, for governors and mayors. Communists rarely win; most winners are young reformers, with no strong party affiliation, running on the platform of economic growth and democratic reform. An occasional good showing by a potential strongman, such as [Vladimir] Zhirinovsky [a right-wing Russian nationalist politician and presidential candidate] is no more than a flash in the pan. The

Russians have had their fill of strongmen and will not tolerate another one. . . .

Russia is rapidly developing into a modern liberal capitalist state. It has been on this road for only a few years, and already has free enterprise, free media, and free elections. Sure, the country has many problems. Many enterprises are inefficient and plagued with outmoded regulations. Some of the new mega-rich are buying up media outlets, trying to control and slant their coverage. Some elections have been marred by claims of restricted access to the media and improper financial support. But these are normal problems of a young democracy.

Periodical Bibliography

The following articles have been selected to supplement the diverse views presented in this chapter. Addresses are provided for periodicals not indexed in the *Readers' Guide to Periodical Literature*, the *Alternative Press Index*, the *Social Sciences Index*, or the *Index to Legal Periodicals and Books*.

Leon Aron	"The Remarkable Rise of Democratic Russia," *Weekly Standard*, April 20, 1998. Available from News America, Inc., 1211 Avenue of the Americas, New York, NY 10036.
Alan Cooperman et al.	"Democracy's Birth Pangs," *U.S. News & World Report*, July 15–22, 1996.
Robert V. Daniels	"Court Politics in Russia," *New Leader*, August 23–September 6, 1999.
John B. Dunlop	"The Wild, Wild East," *Hoover Digest*, Fall 1999. Available from Research and Opinion on Public Policy, Hoover Press, Stanford University, Stanford, CA 94305-6010.
Marco Duranti	"Stains of Red: The Changing Face of Human Rights in Russia and China," *Harvard International Review*, Winter 1998/99.
Jacob Heilbrun	"As the Kremlin Turns," *New Republic*, June 7, 1999.
Johanna McGeary	"The Spy Who Came in from the Crowd," *Time*, April 3, 2000.
Andrew Meier	"Russia's Puppet Master," *Time*, August 23, 1999.
Richard Pipes	"Russia Under Western Eyes," *New Republic*, April 26–May 3, 1999.
Bill Powell	"The End of an Era," *Newsweek*, January 10, 2000.
Dmitry Shlapentokh	"The Permanent Russian Crisis," *Society*, September/October 1999.
Vladimir Shlapentokh	"Will Russia Pass the Democratic Test in 2000?" *Washington Quarterly*, Summer 1999.
Mortimer B. Zuckerman	"Betrayed but Not Broken," *U.S. News & World Report*, September 13, 1999.

CHAPTER 3

Does Russia Pose a Threat to the Rest of the World?

Chapter Preface

For forty years after World War II, the United States viewed Russia—as the central part of the Soviet Union—as the world's leading threat both to U.S. interests and to world peace. In an October 1999 speech at Harvard University, deputy secretary of state Strobe Talbott noted that "when Russia was the core of the Soviet Union and the Warsaw Pact, it posed a threat to us because of its size; its military might; its habit of intimidating and suppressing others; its doctrinal and geopolitical drive to extend its power on a global scale; . . . its hostility to American interests and values. That was the Russia whose strength we confronted and contained."

The collapse of the Soviet Communist dictatorship profoundly changed the nature of Russia's influence on the outside world. Russia's hold on Eastern Europe has been broken, and its once-formidable military machine has shrunk. The size of the Russian armed forces decreased from its peak of more than 5 million members to 1.2 million in 1999. Russia has changed from being a military superpower to an economically weak developing nation—albeit one with nuclear weapons. "Russia has gone from being a strong state to a weak state" concludes Talbott.

However, he and others note that Russia's weaknesses have created their own set of problems. The weakness of the Russian government in enforcing laws has assisted the rise of organized criminals whose activities have expanded to other nations. The debilitated state of Russia's military establishment has caused concern over its ability to control Russia's remaining nuclear arsenal and prevent weapons and materials from falling into the hands of terrorists. The viewpoints in the following chapter examine some of the ways in which Russia might yet remain a threat to its neighbors and to the rest of the world.

| "*For four centuries, Russia has subordinated the well-being of its own population to this relentless outward thrust and threatened all its neighbors with it.*"

Russia Poses an Expansionist Threat

Henry A. Kissinger

From 1969 to 1977 Henry A. Kissinger was the chief foreign policy adviser to Presidents Richard Nixon and Gerald Ford; he remains an influential foreign affairs analyst and commentator. The following viewpoint was written shortly before Russia's June 1996 presidential election in which Boris Yeltsin was reelected over challenger Gennady Zyuganov. In it, Kissinger argues that, regardless of the election's outcome, Russia will inevitably revert to its historical pattern of coping with its domestic problems by aggressively seeking territorial expansion and domination of its neighbors. Kissinger criticizes the foreign policy of the administration of President Bill Clinton for not facing up to Russia's potentially threatening behavior.

As you read, consider the following questions:

1. What are some of the flawed premises of the Clinton administration concerning the Cold War and Russia, according to Kissinger?
2. In Kissinger's opinion, what ideals have motivated Russian expansionism in the past?
3. What is the central challenge for America's foreign policy, according to Kissinger?

Reprinted from Henry A. Kissinger, "Beware: A Threat Abroad," *Newsweek*, June 17, 1996. Reprinted with permission of the author.

In the upcoming [June 1996] Russian election, attention has inevitably focused on the competition between President Boris Yeltsin and Communist Party leader Gennady Zyuganov. But whatever the outcome, America's Russia policy requires an urgent reappraisal. If Zyuganov wins, such a reassessment is inevitable. But a Yeltsin victory, too, would impose a new approach. For even under Yeltsin, Russia is pursuing an increasingly assertive foreign policy, which already opposes American notions of world order in many parts of the world.

The administration will have no choice but to disenthrall itself from the flawed premises of its Russia policy: the conceptual misapprehension of the nature of the Cold War and its overemphasis on personalities. Many policymakers of Clinton's generation hold the view that the United States has its own heavy responsibility for the Cold War, which they believe could have been avoided had the United States pursued a policy of reassurance rather than of confrontation toward the Soviet Union. As a result, Clinton's Russia policy has emphasized domestic reform and psychological engineering. It has concentrated on promoting internal change and on reassuring the Russian leadership rather than seeking to influence Russia's actions outside its borders.

Because Yeltsin is viewed as the guarantor of market economics, democracy and peaceful international conduct, Clinton has attended more summits with him than he has with any other foreign leader and with a far greater show of personal warmth. Though the president has never visited Beijing or invited a Chinese leader to the White House, he has been to Moscow three times and has met with Yeltsin on American soil twice (in addition to meetings at the annual economic summits of industrialized nations). Yet despite these efforts, Yeltsin has embarked on foreign policies which differ only in degree from those urged by Zyuganov, perhaps to stave off the Communists—which have become the largest political party in Russia—or perhaps acting on the basis of his own convictions.

The relationship between market economics and democracy—and between democracy and a peaceful foreign policy—is not nearly so automatic as Washington has postulated. In Western Europe, the process of democratization took centuries and did not prevent a series of catastrophic wars. In Russia, which has no tradition of capitalism and participated neither in the Reformation, the Enlightenment nor the Age of Discovery, this evolution is likely to be particularly ragged. Indeed, the early stages of the process may provide incentives for leaders to mobilize domestic support by appeals to nationalism.

Yeltsin himself is hardly cast in a Jeffersonian mold. Nearly his entire adult life has been devoted to serving the Communist Party—a career to which the gentle-hearted have rarely gravitated. In his rise through its ranks, Yeltsin surely had little exposure to pluralistic principles. And while he was courageous in concluding that the moribund and inefficient Communist Party was doomed, Yeltsin has shown few signs since that democratic values, including acceptance of dissent, are a central part of his value system. In short, equating foreign policy with Russian domestic politics has unnecessarily identified America in the minds of too many Russians with the weird Russian hybrid of black markets, reckless speculation, outright criminal activity and a state capitalism in which big industrial combines are run by their erstwhile Communist managers in the guise of privatization.

This has enabled Russian nationalists and Communists to claim that the entire system is a fraud perpetrated by the West to keep Russia weak. Failure to recognize these realities has caused the administration to emphasize objectives that require a long period of time to evolve, and to neglect matters that need to be shaped in the present.

Our reliance on Yeltsin has lured us into endorsing, if not actually encouraging, such high-handed actions as the military assault on the Russian Parliament and the dismissal of the Russian Constitutional Court—acts difficult to reconcile with democratic pretensions, whatever the provocation. The assumption that Yeltsin must be coddled explains why American high officials, including the president, justified Russian pressures on the newly independent states of the Caucasus as being comparable to American actions in the Caribbean. It is presumably also why they felt it reasonable to compare the Russian military campaign in Chechnya to the American Civil War.

The obsession with participating in Russian domestic politics undermines our ability to conduct a foreign policy geared to the external conduct of the Russian state. Yet it is precisely the external actions of Russia that present the greatest challenge to international stability. And, paradoxically, the very domestic drama of which we have made ourselves too much a party provides some of the incentive for Russian adventurism.

Russia's Dangerous Quest for Power

Undoubtedly Russia's priority policy of reintegrating the Commonwealth of Independent States (CIS) [the former Soviet Union minus the Baltic States]—which it regards as its fundamental task—is a hegemonic one. It is unclear, however, whether the country can sustain this neoimperial project across Europe, the Caucasus, and Central Asia. Local and foreign states compete with Russia or resist it, and Russia itself cannot afford the resources to sustain a new empire. Yet the country's top policymakers have defined this reintegration leading to reunion as the only solution to the profound insecurity that they perceive everywhere. Furthermore, one purpose of this policy is to counter internal separatist trends, a classic imperialist doctrine of launching foreign adventures to divert people from the failed domestic policy agenda. Since foreign policy derives from internal political factors, forces, and struggles, if foreign policy fails, those internal political forces could fail with it. Hence the discrepancy between Russia's ambitions and its means to realize them is the greatest threat to Eurasian security today. Russia might actually gain its goal for a time, but only by ruining itself and its neighbors, an unfathomable but clearly terrifying outcome.

Stephen Blank, *World & I*, November 1997.

Foreign policy has emerged as the deus ex machina for Russia's elite to escape present-day frustrations by evoking visions of a glorious past. Russia has always displayed a unique set of characteristics—especially when compared to its European neighbors. Extending over 11 time zones, Russia (even in its present, post-Soviet form) contains the largest land-mass of any contemporary state. St. Petersburg is closer to New York than it is to Vladivostok, which is in turn closer to Seattle than it is to Moscow. A country of that size ought not to suffer from claustrophobia. Yet creeping expansionism has been the recurring theme of Russian history. For four centuries, Russia has subordinated the well-being of its own population to this relentless outward thrust and threatened all its neighbors with it. In the Russian mind, the centuries of sacrifice have been transmuted into a mission, partly on behalf of security, partly in the service of an alleged Russian superior morality.

In the 19th century, the Russian nationalist writer Mikhail Katkov defined the difference between Western and Russian values as follows: ". . . everything there is based on contractual relations and everything here on faith. A basic dual authority exists there; a single authority here." Similarly, Zyuganov describes Russia as a "special type of civilization" based on "collectivism, unity, statehood"—as compared to the West, infected with "extreme individualism, militant soullessness, religious indifference, adherence to mass culture."

Russia and America have both historically asserted a global vocation for their societies. But while America's idealism derives from the concept of liberty, Russia's sprang from shared suffering and common submission to authority. Everyone is eligible to share in America's values; Russia's have been reserved for the Russian nation, excluding even the subject nationalities of the empire. American idealism tempts isolationism; Russia's has historically prompted adventurist domination.

In pursuit of security, Russia has produced insecurity for all its neighbors. Russia has generally excluded Eastern Europe, the Balkans, the Caucasus and Central Asia from the operation of the balance of power, insisting on dealing with them unilaterally and often by force: in the Treaty of Adrianople in 1829, the Treaty of Unkiar Skelessi in 1833, in the prelude to the Crimean War in 1853, in the Balkan crisis of 1885 and in the period following the second World War. In Manchuria and Korea, prior to the Russo-Japanese War of 1904, it followed a similar strategy. Even when it participated in European alliances, Russia tended to endow them with a missionary quality that justified permanent military intervention in the domestic affairs of other states—from the

Holy Alliance of the early 19th century to the Brezhnev Doctrine of the late 20th century.

Thus Yeltsin's "reformist" foreign minister, Andrei Kozyrev (since dismissed for being too liberal), put forward a Russian right of military intervention in all the countries containing Russian minorities. At a minimum, that includes 14 states of the former Soviet Union (including the Baltic states)—all of them recognized by the United Nations. Two Russian divisions are being maintained on the territory of Georgia, where Russian intervention in a civil war made that country ungovernable until Russian conditions were met. Russia's encouragement of the conflict between Azerbaijan and Armenia has given Moscow a voice in both countries and blackmail potential over Azerbaijan's vast oil reserves. Russian troops participate in the civil war in Tajikistan. Russia refuses to demarcate the borders with Ukraine, a country with a population close to 60 million whose independence Russians seem particularly loath to accept. And Russia is pressuring the oil-producing nations in Central Asia to export their oil only through pipelines running through Russia—claiming for Moscow a stranglehold on one of the largest oil reserves in the world. All this has happened under Yeltsin and at a moment of Russia's maximum weakness.

Russia's simultaneous thrust in all directions runs the risk of repeating the underlying tragedy of its history. No people has sacrificed more for its vision of security and its sense of mission; none has received fewer tangible benefits from it, or has so often turned its fears into self-fulfilling prophecies. Both the czarist and Communist empires collapsed, materially and spiritually exhausted by their overextension. The almost paranoid sense of insecurity is all the less appropriate in the present world, where Russia possesses 20,000 nuclear weapons, making a land attack on it almost inconceivable.

The long-term stakes are high. If Ukraine were to share the fate of Belarus and return to Russian satellite status, tremors would be felt all over Europe. A militarization of diplomacy would be nearly inevitable. A Russian stranglehold on Central Asian oil would provide dangerous blackmail potential during the predictable energy crises of the next [21st] century. Beyond the geopolitical challenges, Russia, in its attempt to regain what it perceives as ancient glories, appears inclined to challenge the U.S. position in the Middle East and to conduct adventurous policies in Asia for no other purpose than to augment its prestige.

Yeltsin has seemed to feel a necessity to balance every high-level American visit with a move in a more nationalist direction. Within days of Clinton's visit to Moscow in 1993, Yeltsin dismissed Yegor Gaidar, the reformer on whom many American hopes had been based. The Chechnya war started shortly after a visit by Vice President Gore. And Clinton had barely left Moscow in April [1996] when Yeltsin betook himself to Beijing and Shanghai, where he signed what had all the appearance of a strategic partnership with China—a maneuver facilitated by the lack of direction in Washington's China policy.

The United States has been far too slow to recognize these challenges. It is only in the last year that Ukraine has received attention commensurate with its political and strategic importance. In Central Asia, American policy seems unable to balance human-rights concerns with a concept worthy of the geopolitical importance of that region. In the Caucasus, flagrant Soviet military or near-military intervention has been met with American silence or by American statements seemingly legitimizing ancient Russian imperial drives.

The most serious lack has been of omission. During the Cold War, America's Atlantic relations were built from West to East, on the basis of a strong Atlantic Alliance and an emerging European Community. Clinton's post–Cold War policy, influenced by the dogmas of the protest movement in which NATO was regarded as a cause of international tensions, seeks to build from East to West. Focused on Russia, it has failed to adapt the Atlantic Alliance to the post–Cold War circumstances. It has offered no vision of a political or economic partnership in the North Atlantic region, or else has consigned such prospects to bureaucratic studies that never seem to have a deadline. This is even more true of NATO expansion—a subject on which administration ambivalence threatens to create a gray zone in Eastern Europe between Germany and Russia, potentially tempting historic

Russian drives to create political and strategic vacuums around its periphery.

Despite mounting evidence in the daily conduct of Russian diplomacy, Washington treats Yeltsin as if he were some tender shoot incapable of withstanding the gusts of a realistic foreign policy. This only encourages Russian leaders to compensate for frustrations at home by appeals to Russian nationalism. If we seek genuine reform in Russia, its leaders must be brought to understand that a return to historic drives will replicate the debacles of the past. For the strategic domination of its neighbors can be achieved only at the cost of permanent tensions with the United States and the West.

Such a policy should be based on a rededication to strengthening the Atlantic relationship. NATO expansion requires a decision, not a study; its absence will tempt an even further thrust to expand Russia's strategic frontiers. (This is certainly the view of literally all the leaders of Eastern Europe.) Even more important, the Atlantic Alliance must deepen its political dimension and extend it to heretofore excluded subjects—Islamic fundamentalism, global energy supplies and other threats to world stability. Finally, the time has come to move the project of a North Atlantic Free Trade area from study committees to the action phase.

As part of such an architecture, Russia could be given an important role in the creation of the new international system. But this presupposes a Russian readiness to stay within its borders. The challenge for America is whether it can assemble a proper balance of incentives and penalties conducive to maintaining such a world order. And this challenge exists whoever wins the Russian election, though it will be more complex after a Zyuganov victory. That is the kind of reform America can—and should—hope to contribute to in the immediate future.

| *"Russia's 'obsession' with prestige is at bottom an admission of weakness."*

Russia Does Not Pose an Expansionist Threat

Stephen Sestanovich

In the following viewpoint, Stephen Sestanovich examines and finds wanting the argument that Russia is a potentially dangerous and expansionist nation bent on subjugating its neighbors. A closer examination reveals that neither Russia's people nor their leaders are motivated to engage in imperialist ventures for reasons of prestige, he contends. At the time this article was first published, Stephen Sestanovich was vice president for Russian and Eurasian affairs at the Carnegie Endowment for International Peace. In 1997 he was appointed ambassador at large to the countries that comprised the former Soviet Union.

As you read, consider the following questions:

1. What four propositions are asserted by what Sestanovich calls the "geotherapists"?
2. What events of the 1996 presidential election does the author use to support his thesis that the Russian public does not care for expansionism?
3. How does Sestanovich respond to the argument that the United States has been "coddling" Russia's leaders?

Excerpted from Stephen Sestanovich, "Geotherapy," *National Interest*, Fall 1996. Copyright © *The National Interest*, no. 45, Washington, D.C. Reprinted with permission.

An ambition, inordinate and immense, one of those ambitions which could only possibly spring in the bosoms of the oppressed, and could only find nourishment in the miseries of a whole nation, ferments in the heart of the Russian people. That nation, essentially aggressive, greedy under the influence of privation, expiates beforehand, by a debasing submission, the design of exercising a tyranny over other nations: the glory, the riches which it hopes for, consoles it for the disgrace to which it submits. To purify himself from the foul and impious sacrifice of all public and personal liberty, the slave, upon his knees, dreams of the conquest of the world.

—The Marquis de Custine, *Russia in 1839*

D uring the Cold War, Americans by and large forgot [French author] Custine, perhaps the grumpiest tourist and most scathing vilifier of Russia who ever wrote. Locked in conflict with a totalitarian state, we thought that the main reason the Soviet Union made trouble for us, and for the world at large, was that it was not a democracy. Take away Bolshevik ideology, the command economy, and the power of the Politburo, and you'd be a long way toward normalcy. Dissolve the Warsaw Pact, slash military spending, give the non-Russian republics their independence, and it would be hard to see what we might fight about. Adopt a constitution, end censorship, respect religious freedom, hold elections, then hold more elections: Could a country that did all these things really be a threat?

Apparently, yes. Political institutions, we are now told, solve much less than was once imagined. They do not address deep psychic and socio-cultural torments, and legions of new Custines have begun to argue that for Russians no torment is deeper than that of being a fallen superpower—unless perhaps it is that of being a fallen superpower while also undergoing the transition to a market economy. In any case, the pain is excruciating and is said to be relieved only by an increasingly belligerent foreign policy, ideally by re-establishment of the Soviet Empire. . . .

The Diagnosis

An exceptionally diverse group of analysts and political commentators subscribes to some version of the diagnosis just set forth. It is embraced by those who were the most ardent critics of the Soviet order and those who are trying their best to restore it, by lowly working journalists and eminent former officials. Despite their differences, they agree on this: Russian imperial consciousness is not dead. To the contrary, writes Richard Pipes, perhaps our greatest historian of Russia, the loss of empire "has produced bewilderment and anguish."

> [N]othing so much troubles many Russians today, not even the decline in their living standards or the prevalence of crime, and nothing so lowers in their eyes the prestige of their government, as the precipitous loss of great-power status.

Anatoly Lukyanov . . . (a leader of the revived Russian Communist Party) seconds this view. "We communists," he has said (this is an admission he would hardly have made in the old days, when good communists despised bourgeois liberties), "always understood perfectly well that the Soviet man, the citizen of Russia, had fewer political rights than a European. But that shortfall was compensated for by the sense of belonging to a great nation, a great state." [Russian president Boris] Yeltsin undid this formula, thereby making Russian democracy vulnerable to a communist revanche.

> He took away that sense of world importance. Any party which takes advantage of this today will be on top. That is why the communists have so many patriotic slogans, slogans of statehood, of nationhood.

The reason that popular government does not mean peace, in short, is that the people don't necessarily want peace; they want to be on top again. As [former secretary of state] Henry Kissinger has put it, "[W]hat passes for Russian democracy too often encourages an expansionist foreign policy." Yeltsin can hardly let the Communists be the only ones to tap the people's mood, so he ends up taking positions that "differ only in degree from those urged by Zyuganov," his Communist challenger in the June [1996] presidential race. As one measure of how domestic political pressures work, Russia is now inclined "to conduct adventurous policies in Asia for no other purpose than to augment its prestige."

For Kissinger, this mad preoccupation with "ancient glories" is no mere election-season phenomenon, but something more durable—and more dangerous. "Foreign policy," he announces, "has emerged as the *deus ex machina* for Russia's elite to escape present-day frustrations by evoking visions of a glorious past." . . .

Toward a Second Opinion

The mere fact that our leading foreign-policy commentators have started to talk like therapists does not, of course, prove that they are wrong. But the mode of analysis is, to say the least, a little unusual—not least because it is so often combined with a vehement insistence that U.S. policy toward Russia must not be, as Henry Kissinger himself put it years ago, "a subdivision of psychiatry." Let us therefore try to verify the diagnosis.

The geotherapists assert the following four propositions. First, that public opinion creates irresistible pressures, to which Russian leaders have to respond, for an expansionist foreign policy. Second, that the Russian elite retains a strong imperial mindset and, in particular, is determined to regain control of the old Soviet Union. Third, that Russian leaders are dangerously preoccupied with questions of prestige and status, and believe that in the past these were their country's proudest asset. And fourth, that the indulgent attitude of the West, and above all the United States, toward Russia, even when it defies us, is making all these pathologies worse. (There are, it has to be said, some differences among the various commentators who argue this case. Some feel more strongly about one proposition than another. But we will be in a better position to decide how seriously to take these little nuances once we see whether even one of the propositions stands up.)

Evaluating these four claims should not be hard. A patient in such terrible shape is going to give daily proof of how much is wrong with him. If Russia really were as sick as this, we should find useful evidence everywhere we look—in domestic struggles for political power, in the conduct of foreign policy, in the strategic concepts embraced by officialdom and the intelligentsia. Do we?

The Traumatized Public

The Russian political system lacks legitimacy; it can't deliver bread, only imperial circuses; expansionism, and expansionism alone, diverts the popular mind from its misery. For symptoms of this problem, we can start with the recent [June 1996] presidential campaign—a political event that in many countries does bring neuroses to the surface. Boris Yeltsin, it should be remembered, ran for reelection on the basis of a dual strategy, and it was often a quite unedifying sight. On those issues where the Communists had him on the defensive, he pandered and dissembled. Hence his promises to pay all back wages and to end the war in Chechnya. At the same time, on those issues where he had *them* on the defensive, Yeltsin turned up the pressure. Hence his lurid evocations of the Communist past and policy initiatives, like his decree on private land ownership, that were meant to frame the election as a choice between politicians who accept the new order and those who don't.

Russians Accept the Collapse of the Soviet Union

Since the collapse of the Soviet Union, there have been dire warnings about impending conflicts between Russia and the former Soviet states because of Russia's inability to accept the loss of its internal empire. Commentators who focused on the rhetoric of certain Russian politicians, Duma members, and commentators—as opposed to the deeds of the Russian government—made dire predictions about a future Russian-Ukrainian conflict or the uprising of the Russian Diaspora in the CIS [Commonwealth of Independent States]. But today, the Russian population, and much of the leadership, have come closer to accepting the breakup of the Soviet Union than at any previous time. And despite the nostalgia for the past, the majority of Russians are unwilling to pay the military or economic costs that any forceful reintegration of the former Soviet Union would entail.

Angela Stent, *Heritage Lectures*, no. 607, April 6, 1998.

Now, where did imperial nostalgia fit into this strategy? Leave aside for the moment the fact that those candidates who put nationalist themes at the center of their campaign lost badly, and that exit polls put the number of voters who were swayed by foreign policy at only 2 percent. If the geotherapists were right about the country's mental state, we should have seen Yeltsin scrambling to prove that he is part of the revisionist patriotic consensus. Instead, we saw him use foreign policy as a tool to demonstrate the differences between himself and the Communists, and to remind voters of what they *don't* want to retrieve from their "glorious" past.

The issue was not simply a matter of rhetoric and mood, but of conflict between the legislature and the executive. On March 15, 1996, the Russian parliament passed two Communist-sponsored resolutions annulling the acts under which the Soviet Union was dissolved in 1991. It declared that the agreement to create a Commonwealth of Independent States (CIS) in place of the USSR "did not and does not have legal force," and charged that the officials who had "prepared, signed, and ratified" this decision had "flagrantly violated the wish of Russia's people to preserve the USSR."

With this bold move, the opposition clearly thought that they had Yeltsin trapped. On the one hand, he could hardly endorse a resolution that personally denounced him. On the other, opposing it would put him on the wrong side of a supposedly supercharged issue. As things turned out, however, the Duma's action proved to be the moment when Yeltsin's campaign got on a winning track for good. It gave the president and his allies their first, best opportunity to persuade voters that the Communists really were bent on restoring the old order. Yeltsin called the resolution "scandalous" and, showing that he had no fear of seeming too attentive to foreign opinion, immediately instructed Russian diplomats to tell other governments that the vote would have no effect.

There is a Moscow witticism that goes: Anyone who does not regret the collapse of the Soviet Union has no heart; anyone who wants to restore it has no brain. The Communists bet that people did not really believe this; they lost the bet. The March 15th resolution and its aftermath certainly put a question mark over the idea that the loss of empire has left Russians in a state of "bewilderment and anguish.". . .

An Imperial Elite?

The fact that reconstituting the Soviet Union has been a bust politically makes it hard to defend the first of the geotherapists' propositions. There is no identifiable pressure from jingoist public opinion that radicalizes all policies until they "differ only in degree." But we can hardly be certain that Russia has sworn off empire just because its people are not imperialists. The elite may have its own, very different aspirations, and lack of popular support will not necessarily keep them from being realized.

This second proposition is a bit harder to put under the microscope. The Russian ruling class is far more diverse than ever before—politically, economically, regionally, generationally, ethnically, and in other ways as well. It is therefore quite artificial to speak of what *the* elite thinks. (This was beginning to be true even in the last years of the Soviet era.) All the same, there are many organizations purporting to express what they claim is a hard-boiled centrist consensus, and none does so more convincingly than the Council on Foreign and Defense Policy (CFDP). The group is a self-styled analog to our own Council on Foreign Relations in its heyday, a comparison made credible by the former's success in bringing together corporate leaders and experts on international affairs. Its members—among whom ambitious insiders, trimmers, and climbers are very well represented—know exactly what is respectable and what is not.

Last winter and spring, the CFDP conducted a series of meetings to discuss a draft report—"theses," they were called—on the issue of integration. The document went through three versions, was greatly expanded, heavily revised, and published in May [1996] under the signature of forty-four bankers, industrialists, journalists, and policy wonks. In its final form (bearing the title, "Will a Union be Reborn?"), it represents the most revealing statement to date of elite opinion about Russia's relations with the other former Soviet states.

The most arresting passage in the CFDP "theses" is the repudiation of the idea of recreating the USSR, which is labeled "an extremely reactionary utopia." Pursuing it, says the report, will only weaken Russia and cause much bloodshed.

> However humiliated the national consciousness of the Russians may be, today Russian society is absolutely unprepared to pay the price of a lot of blood to make up for geopolitical losses.

To be against a restored communist imperium and against bloodshed is not, of course, to be against re-building Russian power. The CFDP believes that the collapse of the Soviet Union left Russia with much less international influence, and it proposes to try to increase it. But how? Bloodshed, it turns out, is just one constraint among many; so is cost.

> The new Russian political and economic elites are oriented more toward economic rather than military-political domination in the territories of the former USSR (the latter is more troublesome and more costly).

"Economic domination," it should be said, doesn't mean a readiness to subsidize poor countries; Russia had its fill of "donorship" in the old days. For the CFDP, the main way to make Russia a "magnet" for the rest of the CIS is through "the successful development of Russia itself, the continuation of democratic and market reforms, and the beginning of an active policy of economic growth."

The CFDP prides itself on being hard-headed and unsentimental, just like the "establishment" (a current Russian vogue word) that it claims to represent. Accordingly, while it favors the goal of "rapprochement and integration," it can't help pointing out the emptiness and stupidity of many proposals for achieving this goal. Russia's relations with the rest of the former Soviet states, for example, should not be over-institutionalized: grand designs are silly. The CFDP "theses" propose instead

> to shift the center of gravity of activities in the space of the former USSR away from the highest level—the establishment of superstructures, the signing of treaties and agreements and the like—to support for specific projects of interaction in the cultural, social and above all economic spheres: the exchange of debt for ownership, the creation of financial-industrial groups, the facilitation of financial transactions, the establishment of joint banks, and so forth.

When it comes to achieving "economic domination," what these hard-headed, unsentimental folks say they want is "a common market for goods and services," and their reasons have a distinctly familiar, unimperial ring. "Openness of markets," they note, "helps to create jobs in all states, alleviating the political and psychological consequences of the disintegration of the USSR."

To be sure, there is also a strong military side to the program. The CFDP definitely supports defense cooperation with CIS states. But it opposes the reflexive broadening of Russia's ambitions and commitments just because it sounds tough and because some neighboring states (for reasons that may not serve Russian interests at all) are willing to cooperate. . . .

The core judgment of the CFDP's report is that, over the long term, closer relations between Russia and the former Soviet states are probably inevitable. But its core recommendation is that Russia should aspire to "leadership, instead of control." Trying to accelerate the process will accomplish nothing, and may even slow things down. . . .

The Matter of Pride

Let us turn to the third element of Russia's allegedly neurotic politics—the preoccupation of its leaders with their country's international status. [Former national security adviser Zbigniew] Brzezinski sees them as "obsessed by the notion that Russia be hailed a great power." And Kissinger, in describing the consequences of Russia's "almost paranoid sense of insecurity," speaks of "adventurous" policies that he claims have no other purpose than "prestige."

In ordinary Russian discourse on foreign policy, the question of prestige does come up in a way that is, at first sight, quite different from what one encounters in an American context. A bureaucratic document produced for President Clinton by the staff of the National Security Council, for example, would not ordinarily speak of protecting the prestige of the United States as a major national interest. Yet last spring [of 1996] *Nezavisimaya Gazeta* devoted three full pages to the publication of just such a document, "The National Security Policy of the Russian Federation, 1996–2000," prepared by the staff of Yeltsin's Security Council. It declared, among other things, that securing and protecting Russia's "international status" were right at the top of its foreign policy goals:

> Russia's most important national interest at a global level is its active and full participation in building a system of international relations in which Russia is assigned a place corre-

sponding in the highest degree to its *potential* political, economic and intellectual significance and its military-political and foreign-economic potential and needs. [emphasis added]

This effort was said to be all the more important because other countries are bent on taking Russia down a peg. For this reason, "maximum efforts must be made to elaborate and use means of effectively countering attempts to weaken [Russia's] international positions and prestige."

How kooky is this? Brzezinski argues that it is extremely destructive. These fits of self-glorification allow Russia to ignore how far it has fallen behind economically. Worse, the inevitable emphasis on past greatness, the nostalgia for a time when the Soviet Union could compete on equal terms with the United States—all this implicitly "legitimizes the Communist Party" and postpones "genuine democratization."

Perhaps. But it is worth looking more closely at the "National Security" document just quoted, for taken as a whole it lends all this talk of prestige a different, indeed opposite, meaning. Brzezinski himself could not ask for a blunter description of Russian reality than one finds here—in, of all places, a public document released on the eve of the presidential election. Far from diverting attention from economic backwardness, Yeltsin's national security staff warns that "it will take several generations before we can compare ourselves with the United States, Japan, Germany, Sweden, France, and so forth." Far from pining for lost superpower equality, the document explicitly "renounces the principle of military-strategic parity with the United States." And far from encouraging the confrontational outlook of old, it says something that will surprise those who know of these matters only what the geotherapists tell them: "Russian citizens must mobilize state structures, the public, the family, and schools to mold a non-aggressive type of individual and a secure society and state." Given all the work that has to be done, Russia's foreign policy bottom-line is a very simple one: It needs to be able to direct its resources to the successful completion of massive internal tasks.

Russians have no trouble understanding the fix they're in, because—unlike us—*they're in it*. They can barely think of anything else. . . .

Russia's "obsession" with prestige is at bottom an admission of weakness. Recall that Yeltsin's "National Security" document, quoted earlier, speaks of the importance of winning an international role based not on Russia's power, but on its *potential*. The determination to protect the country's prestige is not a demand for "adventures" that will show strength, but a hope to get by without being put to the test. Prestige is not a means of dodging the necessary work of democratization, but—if it works—of dodging unnecessary defeats while this work goes on. . . .

The way Russians talk about NATO expansion supports this view of what they mean by prestige. What is most vexing to them about the Western plan to bring the Atlantic Alliance into Eastern Europe is that it dramatizes Russia's loss of standing. It shows Russia to be isolated, without the ability to affect events, without "standing" in the juridical sense—that is, without the right to have a grievance heard in court. Two prominent Russian specialists on America, Aleksei Bogaturov and Viktor Kremeniuk, wrote recently that NATO expansion shows America's complete "disregard for [Russia's] opinion." Russians may be pained by this, they said, but the truth is that Washington "does not have even a shadow of fear over Moscow's possible reaction."

"Coddling" and Its Consequences

Since the end of the Cold War, American presidents—first [George] Bush and now [Bill] Clinton—have treated Russian leaders with exceptional personal courtesy, and with the diplomatic hyperbole embodied in the term "strategic partnership." Russians see this. Bogaturov and Kremeniuk acknowledge "a measure of humanism" in U.S. policy toward their country. The West does not want to "unduly hurt Russia," they say, and will even "spare Russia's self-esteem to the extent possible."

Now the geotherapists are not against politeness as such. What bothers them—and this is their fourth proposition—is the thought that the United States might go beyond cordiality, and actually reshape Western policy to take account of Russian objections (or worse yet, Russian excuses about their domestic political situation). Kissinger scorns "the assumption that Yeltsin must be coddled." Treating him "as if he were some tender shoot," he writes, only encourages more assertive nationalism. Brzezinski sees the same risk in the slow pace of NATO expansion. Delay—which he calls a "disgrace"—"has simply encouraged the current Russian rulers to compete with the extremists." Russia, he insists, is not actually helped by "one-sided deference." What it needs most is a dose of the reality therapy that we gave the Japanese and Germans after the Second World War, which obliged them to make a "clear-cut break" with the past.

This argument is wrong on two separate counts: first, about the course of Russian policy and, second, about the way in which the United States has dealt with defeated or declining powers in the past. Far from "competing" with the Communists in his opposition to NATO expansion, for example, Yeltsin used the pause that the Clinton administration promised him during his re-election campaign to explore possible compromises. The new Russian foreign minister, Yevgeny Primakov, began to say publicly that Russia simply sought assurances that, if NATO took in new members, there would be no extension eastward of the alliance's military structures—in particular, no deployment of its forces or of nuclear weapons. These were precisely the formulas for which his predecessor, Andrei Kozyrev, was routinely denounced as a traitor. So far, no one has called for Primakov's head on a pike. Whatever may explain this latest turn in the story (and the affair is far from over), the one thing that has not happened, in response to American "indulgence," is the radicalization of Russian policy.

As for the issue that most agitates Kissinger—"whether Russia can be made to accept [its current, post-Soviet] borders"—the five-year record shows a huge transformation. When the Soviet Union collapsed at the end of 1991, both Russian and Western analysts identified a series of possible revisionist goals that might appear on the Russian policy agenda at some point—and many people said it would be sooner rather than later. These goals included recovery of Crimea from Ukraine, detaching and absorbing Russian territories from northern Kazakhstan or eastern Ukraine, acquiring some sort of protectorate over Russian communities in Estonia, and so on. What has happened? *Every single one of these issues is less charged, and less urgent, than it was five years ago.* Apart from the occasional Foreign Ministry statement protesting, say, Estonian education policy, it is clearly Russia's aim to downplay all of them. Yet Kissinger continues to argue that the United States has naively encouraged more "assertive" Russian policies. His claims have escalated; Russian policy has not.

A closer look at U.S. policy toward Germany and Japan after 1945 also takes some of the air out of outraged claims that we must not "coddle" Russia. Yes, it was American policy to crush Nazism and Japanese militarism and to prevent their reappearance. But the United States also aimed to build up both countries as allies, and this goal shaped policy toward each of them from the very start of the postwar period. Kissinger's insistence, for example, that the most important test of Russian policy involves acceptance of its borders contrasts sharply with U.S. policy toward Germany during most of the Cold War. West Germany, let us remember, contested the postwar borders of Europe for decades—and with U.S. support. It was only in 1970, a quarter of a century after the war ended, that German claims to a large part of Polish territory were renounced. Throughout this period, moreover, American leaders were properly indignant at the Soviet suggestion that the only reason West Germany would not waive its claims to Poland was that it had not abandoned its Hitlerian dreams.

*"Economic and political upheaval in Russia
has increased the likelihood that . . . security
at nuclear sites will continue to corrode."*

The Proliferation of Russian
Nuclear Weapons Is a Serious
Global Threat

Steve Goldstein

The combination of the breakup of the Soviet Union, the
continued existence of its massive nuclear arsenal, and economic problems in Russia and other former Soviet states has
led numerous observers to express alarm over the possibility
that Russian nuclear weapons might end up in the hands of
terrorist groups or other nations. In the following viewpoint,
Steve Goldstein, a Moscow-based journalist, cites numerous
experts who fear that the risks of nuclear proliferation have
increased in recent years due to economic and political upheavals in Russia and other former Soviet republics, including Kazakhstan and Azerbaijan. Security at Russian nuclear
facilities has been impaired, Goldstein writes, and impoverished Russian officials might be tempted to smuggle nuclear
materials out of the country or sell their nuclear expertise to
the highest bidder.

As you read, consider the following questions:
1. How many Russian weapons scientists have left the
   country, according to Goldstein?
2. What security weaknesses does the author report that
   people have observed at Russian nuclear facilities?

Reprinted from Steve Goldstein, "Leaky Borders Threaten World Security,"
Toronto Star, January 23, 1999. Reprinted with permission of the Knight
Ridder/Tribune Information Services.

"**I**t was an arrest that should have been reason for rejoic-
ing."

Turkish customs agents in Istanbul arrested eight men
Sept. 7 [1998] on charges of smuggling nuclear material
from the former Soviet Union.

Posing as buyers, the agents seized about 5.4 kilograms of
uranium 235 and 7.1 grams of plutonium powder.

The material was being peddled for $1 million (U.S.) by
three men from Kazakhstan, one from Azerbaijan, and four
from Turkey. One suspect was a colonel in the Kazakh army.

While the seizure kept nuclear material out of the hands
of rogue states or terrorists, the incident once again raised
the spectre of terrorists—or an outlaw nation—detonating a
primitive nuclear device.

From small-time hustlers to organized-crime figures, there
are sustained attempts by profiteers to obtain and sell nuclear
material to anyone willing to pay for it.

A Growing Threat

Many nuclear experts say the proliferation threat is greater
now than in recent years.

They say deepening economic and political upheaval in
Russia has increased the likelihood that financially desperate
specialists with access to nuclear material will be tempted to
sell it, or that security at nuclear sites will continue to corrode as fast as the beleaguered economy.

In fact, Russia is perhaps more politically volatile now
than in the early 1990s, with troubling implications for nuclear security: At least 3,000 unpaid and disillusioned Russian scientists with expertise in weapons of mass destruction
have left the country in the last seven years, according to
U.S. intelligence estimates.

Some have gone to rogue nations trying to build nuclear-
weapons programs, such as North Korea, Libya, Iran and Iraq.

The continuing exodus prompted Graham Allison, a Harvard proliferation expert, to conclude . . . that the likelihood
of a nuclear device exploding in the United States has actually increased since the end of the Cold War.

Security at many Russian nuclear facilities is porous, despite U.S.-supplied equipment and expertise, according to

some proliferation experts. U.S. officials estimate that only a quarter of the uranium and plutonium at such facilities is adequately secured. Eighty per cent of the facilities covered by a U.S. security program do not even have portal monitors to detect nuclear material carried through their gates.

There is evidence that Iraqi and Iranian purchase agents are actively seeking nuclear technology and material inside Russia, according to Matthew Bunn, a proliferation expert at Harvard.

Russia's top customs official acknowledges that only about a quarter of the country's 300 border crossings have adequate equipment to thwart nuclear smuggling.

Moscow's central authority is dissipating, salaries are not being paid, and official corruption is endemic, creating conditions conducive to smuggling nuclear materials.

"The economic crisis in Russia is the world's number one proliferation problem," said William Potter, a leading authority on nuclear smuggling.

Potter, who heads the Center for Nonproliferation Studies, a private research institute in Monterey, Calif., recently returned from an inspection trip of five Russian nuclear sites.

He said he found security equipment that had never been installed, highly enriched uranium transported on a canvas-topped truck, and guards who disconnected security sensors after a series of false alarms.

"The situation is desperate," Potter said.

Attempts to Acquire Nuclear Material

The September seizure in Turkey is one of several disturbing recent attempts to acquire, smuggle or sell nuclear material.

In February [1999], Italian police arrested 14 members of the Italian Mafia on charges of attempting to sell uranium fuel rods. It was the first documented case of an organized-crime group attempting to sell nuclear material.

On Nov. 4 [1998], a federal indictment charged that Saudi exile Osama bin Laden and members of his terrorist organization, al Qaeda, "made efforts to obtain the components of nuclear weapons," presumably for terrorist purposes.

In December [1998], despite the bombings of Iraq by U.S. and British forces, there was evidence that Saddam Hussein lacked only fissile material—material able to fuel an atomic reaction—to build nuclear weapons.

The week the bombings ended, David Albright of the private Institute for Science and International Security in Washington and Khidir Hamza, a former Iraqi nuclear-weapons scientist, reported that Iraq could rapidly make a nuclear weapon once it acquired fissile material.

Reprinted by permission of Mike Luckovich and Creators Syndicate.

Former U.N. weapons inspector Scott Ritter earlier had reported to the CIA that Iraq had completed the shells of four 20-kiloton nuclear devices.

"If Iraq acquires plutonium or HEU (highly enriched uranium) from Russia, Saddam Hussein could have nuclear weapons within a matter of months," Albright said.

Uranium enriched to more than 90 per cent is considered weapons-grade.

Terrorist Groups

For years, U.S. officials took solace in the belief that there were no active buyers in the black market, even as prospective sellers stole uranium and plutonium from sites in Russia. The emergence of aggressive terrorist groups such as bin Laden's al Qaeda and Japan's doomsday cult Aum Shinri Kyo (Aum Supreme Truth), coupled with the recent diversion cases, has pierced that sense of security.

In addition, experts report several cases in which smugglers tried to sell material that is not weapons-usable, such as beryllium and cesium, but is still harmful and thus suitable for terrorism.

In late 1995, Chechen separatists locked in a war with Russia threatened to blow up radioactive materials they had buried in a park in Moscow.

Police found a vial of cesium buried near a footpath in popular Izmailovsky Park. Cesium causes radiation poisoning if not handled properly.

Russia's nuclear inventory includes about 30,000 nuclear warheads, 1,050 metric tons of weapons-usable, highly enriched uranium, and up to 200 metric tons of separated plutonium contained within weapons or available for weapons. At a minimum, the material is enough to build 120,000 nuclear weapons, assuming 4 kilograms of plutonium and 12 kilograms of highly enriched uranium for each weapon.

The amount of nuclear material needed to build a crude bomb is so small that smugglers have hidden it in their trousers.

Retired Russian Gen. Alexander Lebed has described Russian nuclear "suitcase bombs" small enough to fit inside a briefcase. Authorities do not know how much nuclear material has been stolen but never reported.

"What has surfaced," said Rens Lee, author of *Smuggling Armageddon*, "may just be a small amount of what has been stolen."

Missing Nuclear Material

In some cases, material is reported stolen but never recovered.

In 1996, 900 grams of enriched uranium 235 vanished from Tomsk Polytechnic University in western Siberia. Because of poor accounting and control procedures, Russian officials do not know whether the material was stolen or accidentally mixed with other nuclear fuel.

How does the material reach other countries? One persuasive theory is that smugglers no longer attempt to pierce relatively tightly controlled European borders, but instead probe the poorly protected southern border of the former Soviet Union. In fact, the southern tiers of newly independent, ex-Soviet nations share a 7,100-kilometre border with Iran, Turkey, Afghanistan and China.

The September sting in Turkey is considered Exhibit A among experts concerned that nuclear material is leaking across these southern borders. It was the third reported seizure of uranium by Turkish officials since 1994.

One serious case that has been reported is the disappearance of 2 kilograms of highly enriched uranium—enriched to more than 90 per cent—in the breakaway Abkhaz Republic in Georgia.

The material had been stored at the I.N. Vekua Physics and Technology Institute in Sukhumi and had been last inventoried in 1992.

Because Sukhumi is in Abkhazia, the institute is no longer under the direct control of Georgia's authorities.

At the request of Georgia's government, the International Atomic Energy Agency and the Russian Ministry of Atomic Energy attempted to conduct an inventory of the institute but were prevented by continuing strife.

In December 1997, a Russian team finally gained access to the facility.

The storage site had been broken into and all available uranium had been stolen, although other radioactive material was still present.

Russia has no idea how long the material has been missing or where it has gone.

"There is absolutely no evidence that nuclear weapons . . . are leaking from Russia."

The Threat of Russia-Sponsored Nuclear Proliferation Is Exaggerated

William C. Martel

William C. Martel is an associate professor of international relations and Russian studies at the Air War College at Maxwell Air Force Base in Alabama. In the following viewpoint, he argues that the notion that Russian "loose nukes" are leaking to terrorists or rogue states is a myth with little basis in reality. No evidence has surfaced proving that such nuclear proliferation has actually occurred, he contends. Martel asserts that Russians might have a vested interest in promulgating the "loose nukes" myth in order to prod the United States to spend millions of dollars assisting Russia's nuclear complex—money that might be better spent on U.S. nuclear weapons inspection capabilities.

As you read, consider the following questions:

1. What three reasons does Martel give for criticizing the "loose nukes" myth?
2. What political reaction has been created within Russia concerning American subsidies to Russia's nuclear security, according to the author?
3. What steps should the United States take to combat nuclear proliferation, according to Martel?

Reprinted from William C. Martel, "Puncturing the 'Loose Nukes' Myth," *USA Today*, March 1997. Reprinted with permission.

S ince the Soviet collapse, the American public has been bombarded with the "loose nukes" myth. It maintains that Russian nuclear weapons and materials are leaking to terrorists or rogue states such as Libya, Iran, Iraq, or North Korea.

Despite warnings from the Clinton Administration; in the last [104th] Congress from Senators Sam Nunn (D.-Ga.) and Richard Lugar (R.-Ind.); the Russian government; editorial pages; the Central Intelligence Agency; a General Accounting Office report released in March, 1996; and testimony before the Senate Government Affairs Subcommittee that same month, the "loose nukes" myth survives. Nevertheless, it is not credible, for several reasons:

Fissile materials are not leaking from Russia. The myth is that bomb-grade materials—highly enriched uranium or plutonium—are leaking out of Russia. In fact, there is no evidence of any significant leakage of fissile material.

Despite media reports since 1992, low-level radioactive isotopes smuggled out of Europe—notably from Germany and the Czech Republic—can not be used to produce nuclear weapons. The occasional leakages of fissile material involve such minuscule amounts—in fractions of grams, not the kilograms necessary—that building nuclear weapons is not technically possible.

Nuclear weapons are not leaking from Russia. Most importantly, there is absolutely no evidence that nuclear weapons themselves are leaking from Russia. Rumors in 1992 that Kazakhstan sold two tactical nuclear weapons to Iran have been discredited by U.S., Russian, Iranian, and Kazak officials.

The real threat to U.S. interests is the sale of nuclear technology to rogue states. For example, Russia continues its $1,000,000,000 nuclear reactor sale to Iran, despite tremendous pressure from the Clinton Administration. Iran is more likely to develop nuclear weapons with the reactor being rebuilt by Russian technicians than from "loose nukes."

No Brain Drain

There is no "brain drain" of Russian nuclear scientists. In the early 1990s, there were claims that Russian nuclear scientists would emigrate to sell their skills to the highest bidders. Aside from unsubstantiated, sporadic rumors of their pres-

ence in North Korea and China, there is no evidence of unemployed Russian scientists building nuclear weapons for
rogue states. Although there is no exodus to stop, the U.S.
subsidizes the International Science and Technology Center
in Moscow to keep unemployed Russian nuclear scientists
off the streets.

To maintain the integrity of Russia's nuclear complex, the
U.S. spends roughly $400,000,000 per year on the Nunn-
Lugar initiative, also known as the Cooperative Threat Reduction program. Moreover, Russia is not broke. Despite economic hardship, it invests billions in defense modernization.

How the U.S. Department of Energy Assists Russia's Nuclear Security

The Department of Energy is installing advanced U.S. material protection technology to increase [the] security [of Russian nuclear materials] at sensitive sites in conjunction with
the Russian Federation. Physical protection devices, such as
motion detectors, cameras, and vibration sensors have been
placed in rooms containing weapons-grade material. Vibration sensors, placed on doors and walls, are necessary to prevent a determined thief from breaking into a room using a
drill or heavy-duty saw. Doors and windows were hardened
to delay intruders, and sensors and cameras were added to
thwart theft or diversion of nuclear materials. At the Belo-
yarsk Nuclear Power Plant (BNPP) in Zarechny, a vehicle
and personnel portal were upgraded to include a motorized
vehicle gate and a vehicle entrapment area. The response
force at BNPP and Sverdlovsk Branch of the Research and
Development Institute of Power Engineering (SF-NIKIET)
received upgraded radio communication equipment that allows them to communicate and respond more effectively.

U.S. Department of Energy, *M2 Presswire*, April 28, 1998.

Finally, doubts about the security of nuclear weapons facilities are puzzling. My own visits to sensitive Russian defense enterprises and military installations reveal very tight
security, yet we are told of nuclear weapons and materials
leaking out of the nuclear complex. One wonders if the
spending of U.S. millions for the security of Russia' s nuclear
materials may not promote as much mischief as it is designed
to prevent. One wonders if there is an incentive for the Rus-

sians to overlook or sustain some kind of "modest" leakage in nuclear materials so that alarms will remain on and coffers will stay open.

Governmental, military, and intelligence officials in Russia vehemently deny that Russia is the source of radioactive isotopes found in Europe. Aleksandr Lebed, the former national security chief, pointedly maintained that nuclear security is Russia's, not the U.S.'s, concern. A senior representative of the Russian Duma, in an interview with the author, argued that public attention to the economic plight of the nuclear complex "will create the very problems that we want to avoid." American funds are fueling nationalist fires in Russia, as Russians conclude that U.S. spending masks condescension about their nation's ability to secure its nuclear weapons and materials.

There is growing skepticism on Capitol Hill about using U.S. taxpayer dollars to subsidize Russian nuclear security when domestic programs are being cut to balance the Federal budget. Despite Clinton Administration opposition, Congress sliced Nunn-Lugar funds from $400,000,000 to $377,000,000—a six percent reduction. Only the prestige of Sam Nunn and Richard Lugar prevented Congress from zeroing out all outlays.

Alternative Steps

Administration worries about Russian nuclear leakage are not supportable. As the Clinton Administration reorganizes itself for a second term [1996–2000], there are more productive steps for addressing the real problem of proliferation. A U.S. policy for helping states attain security without nuclear weapons has three components:

First, the real dilemma is "loose salesmen," rather than "loose nukes." Hence, we must restrict the sale or transfer of nuclear technologies to rogue states that create independent capabilities for producing nuclear weapons. Weak international inspection regimes for the transfer of nuclear technologies and materials must be strengthened.

Second, the U.S. should develop independent capabilities to monitor and prevent the sale or transfer of nuclear technologies and materials. The $400,000,000 spent each year on Russia could help the U.S. bolster its own inspection capabilities. America must strengthen its intelligence and technological resources to detect and prevent the surreptitious movement of terrorist weapons and materials into U.S. ports and airports. This policy fits much more directly with the interests of the American people.

Third, the U.S. program of subsidizing Russia's nuclear security is no substitute for Russian action. Senior Russian officials are adamant about their ability to manage nuclear materials on Russian soil. The U.S. could create a stronger relationship with Russia, while simultaneously promoting free-market reforms and eliminating $400,000,000 spent per year on nuclear security.

"Russia's Mafia godfathers have now graduated from small-time extortion and protection schemes . . . to become world-class crime czars."

The Russian Mafia Is a Serious Threat to the United States

Part I: Stephen Handelman; Part II: James Kim

The following two-part viewpoint examines organized crime in Russia and its effects both within and outside Russia's borders. In Part I, Stephen Handelman chronicles the rise of Russia's organized crime and argues that Russian crime groups are becoming extremely powerful and sophisticated. Handelman is a journalist and author of *Comrade Criminal: Russia's New Mafiya* (Yale University Press). In Part II, *USA Today* reporter James Kim records the views of experts on the actions of Russian crime figures within the United States. Russian criminals are infiltrating U.S. banks and companies in order to carry out their schemes, he argues, and they pose a significant threat to U.S. society.

As you read, consider the following questions:

1. What two distinct categories of Russian crimelords does Handelman identify?
2. How much capital flight has Russia experienced since 1991, according to Handelman?
3. What patterns of Russian criminal activity in the United States does Kim describe?

I

The director of a small, lucrative Moscow real estate brokerage firm once explained to me why he avoided paying taxes. It wasn't just the high rates, then approaching 40%, he said. What particularly worried him was the requirement to provide a statement of income to state bureaucrats, whom he feared would pass on the information to local Mafia lords. He knew what would happen then—a demand for an increase in the protection rate he was already paying to the same armed groups in order to remain alive in the city's Wild West economy.

That was in 1993, less than a year after the introduction of "capitalism" to the new Russian state. Things have only gotten more sophisticated since then. This week [in September 1999], the House Banking Committee, chaired by Iowa Rep. Jim Leach, will look into allegations that organized-crime groups and government officials have laundered billions of dollars in Russian assets through Western banks. But where most of those reports have concentrated on the remarkable ease with which the money crossed international borders, the key problem has usually been overlooked: the collusion between criminals and government bureaucrats that lies at the heart of the Russian failure to live up to the promise of postcommunist democracy.

Not a Secret

The emerging financial and political power of Russian organized crime was never a secret. Anyone who lived in Russia in the late 1980s and early 1990s knew that the astonishing explosion of entrepreneurship that accompanied the gradual weakening of Communist Party control had a dark side. Firebombings of cooperative restaurants, brutal murders, kidnappings and mysterious bomb blasts suggested even then that a force was already at work replacing the tyrannical state with a terrifying dictatorship of racketeers.

More than 80% of Moscow businesses were already paying protection money or forced to engage "silent partners" by 1993, and in that same year, government authorities acknowledged that organized crime accounted for 30% to 40% of Russia's annual turnover in goods and services. Nevertheless, the Western response to the contagion reflected the official Russian government line: Corruption was merely the price to be paid for the chaos of a transition economy. Eventually, the reformers would gain control, and channel all this criminal energy to productive uses.

How wrong we were. Russia's Mafia godfathers have now graduated from small-time extortion and protection schemes developed in the chaos of a black-market economy to become world-class crime czars. They are likely to dominate 21st-century transnational crime the way Microsoft dominates information technology. And these Armani-clad, computer-savvy, Russian-accented Bill Gates wannabes could not have done it without the collusion, both witting and unwitting, of governments in the East and West.

In the current political debate in the U.S. over "who lost Russia," it's worth taking a closer look at who these CEOs of Russian crime really are, and how they got that way. Hollywood would have a difficult time casting them, since they don't quite fit the usual preconceptions of mafia overlords. There are two distinct categories.

The first is almost as old as the Russian state: the robber brigand of Russian folklore who lives outside and in opposition to the czar's rule. Shortly before the 1917 Russian Revolution, such men, known as *Vory v Zakonye* (Thieves in Law) were taken as role models by Marxist revolutionaries who admired their skill in organizing paramilitary societies and adopted their modus operandi of preying on the rich and terrorizing government functionaries.

Thieves' societies operated with varying degrees of success through the Soviet era. Many Vory considered themselves "dissidents" to the Soviet system and achieved a quiet cult status underground, but with the liberalization of the Soviet economy in the 1960s they became crucial players in the black-market economy, often striking up informal partnerships with local government officials and security organs. In some southern Russian towns, the local Vor had more power and authority than the Communist Party secretary. Except for the distinctive tattoos that identified his status to the cognoscenti, he was to all appearances just another elderly pensioner.

With the collapse of the Soviet state, many of these men and the organizations they led emerged from obscurity. They represented one of the few "institutions" left standing on the vast territories of the old federation, and they commanded a huge source of free capital that could be invested in the Russian economy. Their only competition in this regard was the Communist Party itself, whose enormous reserves of cash were being quietly transferred to the newly established banks, brokerages and businesses. The two principal sources of financial capital in postcommunist Russia found a mutual interest in reviving their old partnership, but it did not happen smoothly. The jockeying for control over the spoils of the old communist state came with a murderous internecine violence not seen in Russia since the civil war of the 1920s. Many Vory lost their lives in mob-style assassinations; others adapted to the new world.

Don Wright ©Tribune Information Services. All rights reserved.
Reprinted with permission.

Out of this synergy emerged the second category of crime bosses, the so-called Authorities. Sleeker, more profit-oriented and better-educated, they came from those sectors of the population that had developed mutually beneficial links with the classic underworld in the Soviet era while being sophisticated in the ways of the larger world: former KGB operatives, former Communist Party and Komsomol officials, state-enterprise managers, smugglers. They were as indistinguishable from the population as the Vory of old, except now they looked like the new bankers, politicians and government officials they were. To coin a phrase, they were Comrade Criminals—masters of white-collar intrigue who were able to fuse the ruthless entrepreneurial tactics of the old criminal gangs with the networks of the Communist Party *nomenklatura* elite. It is this fusion of ruthlessness, financial skill and international sophistication that has made them a unique global force.

The problem was—and still is—to distinguish them from the legitimate entrepreneurs and honest officials of New Russian society. The amorphousness of their control and wealth has made it hard for ordinary Russians, much less Western observers, to know who is who—or, more aptly, who is behind what. What makes the picture even more confusing is that the crime CEOs themselves are not necessarily figures of abuse in many parts of Russia. The gangs' folkloric claim to be the embodiment of Russian national ideals, religious virtue and state order has made them attractive to ultranationalist groups, young people and many others who feel victimized by the inequities of Russian economics. In 1998 the Moscow press reported that one provincial governor openly courted a local mobster (who was already contributing to major charities) to help pay the salaries of workers in his region.

What's Illegitimate?

To make matters even more complicated for outsiders, the line between legitimate and illegitimate economic activity has never been clear. The "democratic" economic reforms of the 1990s were instituted in the same way as state-led initiatives throughout Russian history: with a minimum of debate and with no plausible infrastructure to govern their enforcement. If Russia's criminal bosses exploited the legal vacuum, so did ordinary Russians. The Moscow real-estate broker sent his money abroad as eagerly as the crime bosses who were receiving protection payments from him and the government bureaucrats who were getting a cut of the profits. An estimated $200 billion has left Russia since 1991, and no small part of that comes from the "legitimate" earnings of ordinary Russians who have, under the circumstances, responded rationally to a system in which only the fittest survive.

Money laundering—if that is even the proper description for the avalanche of funds that now flit back and forth between Russia and the West—is a symptom of what ails Russia rather than the disease itself. Our continuing inability to understand and respond to the sources of Russian "criminal behavior" and corruption ensures that the disease will worsen—and infect us.

II

Russian organized crime activity in the USA has two faces—when visible at all.

No matter what form it takes, such crime is a serious problem, experts and former investigators agree. "Crime is the fastest-growing industry in Russia today," says Frank Cilluffo of the Center for Strategic & International Studies. And now, it is being exported.

In the USA, the first wave of Russian-linked crime involved prostitution, gasoline and insurance scams, extortion and general racketeering, stereotypical low-level "mob" stuff, experts say. In this arena, law enforcement authorities claimed a key victory in 1996, when Vyacheslav Ivankov, considered a major Russian organized crime figure, was convicted on two counts of extortion against two Wall Street brokers.

New Forms

Investigators are continuing to examine possible crimes that are of a white-collar, financial nature—only far more sophisticated. The latest revelation: The possible involvement of the Bank of New York, the 16th-largest in the USA. Law enforcement authorities say the bank may have been used to launder as much as $10 billion for Russian criminal organizations.

The *New York Times* linked the dubious activity to Semyon Yukovich Mogilevich, allegedly one of the most prominent Russian crime lords. A detailed *Village Voice* article called Mogilevich the most dangerous mobster in the world.

Many experts say the Bank of New York episode, if true, is one of the largest money-laundering attempts ever through a U.S. bank. "Mind-boggling," says Howard Abadinsky, a criminal justice professor at St. Xavier College.

Former law enforcement officials and other experts say this new wave of crime marks a step up in sophistication. In testimony before Congress in 1997, Louis Freeh, director of the FBI, said that Russian groups' use of computer and encryption technology is formidable. And that makes them more of a challenge to law enforcement officers.

Enemy Within

New Russian organized crime chiefs "are an international threat to the United States," Abadinsky says. "They are able to find all the weak links in American capitalism."

The pattern of the Russian crime wave is clear, says Vladimir Brovkin, a professor at American University's Transnational Center for Crime and Corruption. Typically, highly educated Russians set up or infiltrate Western companies, he says. Then they use the company to launder money or carry out other criminal activity.

One example: YBM Magnex, a Newton, Pa., industrial magnet maker. In June [1999], the company pled guilty to conspiracy to commit securities and mail fraud. At the time, prosecutors said they were also considering charges against an unnamed individual active in the firm's operations, one they consider a major organized crime figure in the former Soviet Union.

Global Scope

Increasingly, Russian groups operate far-flung global enterprises. The Center for Strategic & International Studies has found that they operate in 58 countries. They have forged links with Colombian drug lords, the Italian Mafia and many European groups, according to published reports. They are also active in the Caribbean, particularly on such islands as Montserrat and Antigua, says Charles Intriago, publisher of Miami-based newsletter *Money Laundering Alert*.

The scope of such activity often seems brazen. According to court documents that were widely publicized, U.S. authorities in Miami uncovered an attempt by local strip-joint owner Ludwig Fainberg to broker a deal between Russian and Colombian crime groups. Fainberg was offering a submarine, once owned by the Soviet Navy, to transport cocaine to southern California. Fainberg was subsequently indicted on federal racketeering charges.

The episode also illustrates the structure of Russian crime groups, which is quite different from the old Italian mob, former investigators say.

Russian crime groups are much less hierarchical. Various entities often come together only for a specific project. "They don't neatly fit the pattern of a godfather and foot soldiers," Cilluffo says. "It's almost a business proposition. They're good networkers. A group has to be able to add value."

Economic Roots

Since the Soviet Union fell in 1991, Russia and its satellites have struggled to spawn capitalist economies. So it may also be a question of economic policy, says Brovkin. "Some say the Russian government has not created an environment for normal business. There is no law and order. Tax rates are usurious. That is all true."

As Russia-style capitalism took root, gangsters quickly formed bonds with government bureaucrats and corporate chieftains, blurring the lines between legal and illegal businesses. In a February 1997 national address, President Boris Yeltsin acknowledged the problem, saying the "criminal world has openly challenged the state and launched into an open competition with it."

The success of crime groups in Russia likely means that more money will be sent abroad to avoid taxes and be laundered, continuing the problems here. "You have massive capital flight," Brovkin says. "So it is a massive problem."

"The facts do not support the proposition that Soviet émigrés currently constitute an organized crime threat to the United States."

There Is No Russian Mafia Threat in the United States

James O. Finckenauer and Elin J. Waring

James O. Finckenauer is a professor of criminal justice at Rutgers University. Elin J. Waring is a sociology professor at the Herbert H. Lehman College, City University of New York. The following viewpoint is excerpted from their book *Russian Mafia in America*, a study of Russian organized crime based on their national survey of law enforcement agencies and the work of the Tri-state Soviet Émigré Organized Crime Project, an investigative effort of the states of New York, New Jersey, and Pennsylvania. Finckenauer and Waring conclude that while Russian criminals do operate in the United States, they do not constitute an organized crime phenomenon as traditionally defined. The "Russian mafia," in short, is a stereotype with limited basis in reality.

As you read, consider the following questions:

1. Why, in the opinion of Finckenauer and Waring, have the mass media been quick to identify a Russian mafia problem?
2. In what respects do Russian criminals fail to meet Diego Gambetta's definition of "mafia," according to the authors?
3. What kinds of crimes are Russians most likely to commit, according to Finckenauer and Waring?

Wanting to make familiar what is unfamiliar is a generally acknowledged phenomenon. One result of this is a tendency on the part of some in law enforcement and the media to too readily adopt simplistic, stereotyped perceptions. This has certainly been true in the case of Soviet émigré crime, where the term *Russian mafia* has been loosely applied. As with all stereotypes, this one serves the purpose of simplifying what is otherwise a complex and varied subject. It provides a shorthand characterization that enables law enforcement to communicate among themselves and with the media. The media, in turn, then communicate to the public using this same generally understood term.

[Freelance writer] Scott Anderson referred to this phenomenon in a 1995 magazine article about Yaponchik [Vyacheslav Ivankov, a Russian criminal arrested by the FBI in 1995]. He said that law enforcement, journalists, and gangsters operate in a complexly symbiotic shadow world where it is difficult to separate myth from reality because myth and reality are the same thing. "Ivankov," said Anderson, "was a mafia godfather because it served everyone's interest that he be one. It gave the media a frame, a way to personalize stories about a complex issue. It gave the FBI a symbol to take down, a tool with which to convince the Russian émigré community that justice would prevail." The label *Russian mafia* offers a convenient hook for understanding but at the same time sensationalizes matters so as to pique interest. It thus serves both law enforcement and media interests.

[Criminologist] Lydia Rosner offered three answers to why the Russian mafia is sexy. First, she said, there is a need for a substitute in the wake of the fading of the Italian mafia mythology. In addition to the discrediting of the mafia myth, the real Cosa Nostra [American Mafia] was badly battered during the past decade, as major figures like John Gotti were sent off to prison. The role played by the Italian mafia myth, if there continued to be such a role, thus had to be assumed by another entity, and the Russians were an attractive alternative. A second answer, Rosner says, is that the lingering "evil empire" image makes it "sexy to read about immigrants from the former Soviet Union who are involved in criminal activities on a grand scale." The cold war and nearly fifty

years of competition with the Soviet Union gave Soviets a special status in the eyes of Americans. This special status makes us both more attentive and suspicious of them. Finally, says Rosner, "The sexy Russian Mafia provides journalists and their readers with a relatively unthreatening, European model of crime." By this she seems to mean that just as there was an alien conspiracy belief underlying the Italian mafia myth—a belief that allowed us to attribute our organized crime problem to foreign devils—so too there is now an alien conspiracy belief involving the Russian mafia. According to Rosner, this is a model that is "appealingly seductive, although quite inaccurate." To understand what makes it inaccurate, we go back first to [Sicilian Mafia expert] Diego Gambetta. Gambetta offered a very precise and narrowly focused definition of *mafia* that not only distinguishes it from organized crime but clears up a great deal of the confusion about what really constitutes a mafia. He said that a mafia is a specific economic enterprise, "an industry which produces, promotes, and sells private protection." Mafiosi deal in neither legal nor illegal goods. They are not entrepreneurs. Their only product is protection. This protection becomes necessary and desirable in a marketplace where there are "unstable transactions" and where "trust is scarce and fragile."

The mafia protection is a real service, and mafiosi do not merely practice extortion. It is the fact that people who find it in their interest to buy mafia protection may willingly purchase this service that makes it unlike extortion. Honor flows to those mafiosi who have a reputation for supplying credible protection. According to Gambetta, the world is full of violent entrepreneurs, Russians included. Mafiosi, however, are different. "If we confuse them with entrepreneurs, no matter how vicious, engaged in manipulating the market to their own advantage, then the Mafia evaporates, and we are left with nothing to define it except . . . nebulous distinctions."

Gambetta's definition does not fit the criminally active Russians in the United States. . . . The ex-Soviets are criminal entrepreneurs and extortionists. Rather than providing a protection service for market transactions, they are preda-

tors in the marketplace. Little honor and respect—except that inspired by fear—are shown to them by members of the émigré community. This is clear from the interviews in and around Brighton Beach [a New York City neighborhood heavily populated with Russian immigrants].

A Creation of the Media

The idea of an American-based Russian Mafia is largely a creation of the media and law enforcement. The symbolism and romance attached to the term *mafia*—and the level of law enforcement response it seems to call for—have given this idea a receptive audience in the United States; but it has little basis in fact.

James O. Finckenauer and Elin J. Waring, *Russian Mafia in America*, 1998.

Russian émigré crime is not a mafia or mafialike because it has not moved beyond simply engaging in crimes that are sometimes well organized. . . . [Regarding] conditions that encourage the development of mafias, it is obvious that these conditions do not prevail in the contemporary United States. Government at the local, state, and federal levels has not abdicated its legitimate power. These governments have not left a power vacuum to be filled by other authority, such as a Russian mafia. Government here is also not excessively bureaucratized or especially prone to corruption. Except for rumors, there is little evidence that Russians are corrupting American officials. In addition, the actual and potential illegal markets available do not lend themselves to domination and monopolization by these Russians. Indeed, in the most lucrative of the illegal markets—drugs and gambling—there is considerable competition from a variety of criminal organizations that are sufficiently powerful to make it impossible for Russian criminals to force them out. We found no evidence that any Russian criminal organization (or organizations) controls drugs, gambling, prostitution, or extortion, in Brighton Beach—where, if anywhere, such control would be most likely. It is our judgment that there is no Russian mafia in the United States. . . .

The most highly organized form of crime in the former Soviet Union was white-collar corruption. It was tied to the black market and the shadow economy. Given this tradition, we would expect Soviet émigrés who come to the United States seeking criminal opportunities to have had little involvement in such staples of traditional organized crime as gambling, drugs, and prostitution. Instead, we would expect to find them experienced in crimes of deception. And, indeed, that is what our empirical evidence from the Tri-state Project database and the national law enforcement survey shows. Those data clearly demonstrate Soviet émigrés' involvement in crimes of deception. For example, of those U.S. law enforcement agencies that reported contact with Russians, 53 percent reported fraud crimes, 32 percent reported money laundering, and 31 percent reported drug crimes. Typical organized crimes such as extortion, racketeering, prostitution, and loan sharking were reported by only 19 percent, 17 percent, 12 percent, and 5 percent, respectively. Among these law enforcement agencies there is obviously very limited support for the contention that there is a serious Russian organized crime problem in the United States. . . .

Based on all the information available to us, we conclude that the facts do not support the proposition that Soviet émigrés currently constitute an organized crime threat to the United States. Increased immigration and new criminal opportunities may change the nature of émigré crime, but the very nature of these criminal activities may continue to militate against either a need or a desire to adopt a more traditional organized crime structure, such as La Cosa Nostra.

Whatever form or forms may arise, we are confident that they will not constitute a Russian mafia. It is ironic that so many émigrés from the former Soviet Union feel themselves tainted by the stereotype of a Russian mafia that is neither Russian nor a mafia. Most are not opportunists or criminal entrepreneurs wanting only to take advantage of others. But those who are will be the objects of our continuing attention.

Periodical Bibliography

The following articles have been selected to supplement the diverse views presented in this chapter. Addresses are provided for periodicals not indexed in the *Readers' Guide to Periodical Literature*, the *Alternative Press Index*, the *Social Sciences Index*, or the *Index to Legal Periodicals and Books*.

Shlomo Avineri	"Setting Sun," *New Republic*, March 20, 1995.
Joseph R. Biden Jr.	"Maintaining the Proliferation Fight in the Former Soviet Union," *Arms Control Today*, March 1999.
Yaroslav Bilinsky	"Russian Foreign Policy in Search of a Nation," *Orbis*, Fall 1997.
Stephen Blank	"Dreams of a Salesman: Russia and the Proliferation of Weapons of Mass Destruction, *World & I*, October 1998. Available from 3400 New York Ave. NE, Washington, DC 20002.
Raymond Bonner	"Russian Gangsters Exploit Capitalism to Increase Profits," *New York Times*, July 25, 1999.
Matthew Evangelista	"Russia's Fragile Union," *Bulletin of the Atomic Scientists*, May/June 1999.
Robert I. Friedman	"White Collar and Dangerous," *New York Times*, August 27, 1999.
Harper's	"Back to the U.S.S.R.?" July 1996.
Jacob Heilbrun	"Clean Break," *New Republic*, September 28, 1998.
Michael Hirsh	"The Gangster State," *Newsweek*, September 6, 1999.
David Hoffman	"Is Russia's Center of Power Collapsing?" *Washington Post National Weekly Edition*, March 8, 1999. Available from Reprints, 1150 15th St. NW, Washington, DC 20071.
Michael Krepon	"Missile Defense: Not Such a Bad Idea," *Bulletin of the Atomic Scientists*, May/June 1999.
Chandler Rosenberger	"Russian Roulette," *National Review*, January 26, 1998.
Brett Wagner	"Nukes for Sale," *Wall Street Journal*, September 9, 1999.

CHAPTER 4

What Should U.S. Foreign Policy Be Toward Russia?

Chapter Preface

The United States enjoyed a period of friendly relations with Russia in the first years following the breakup of the Soviet Union in 1991. U.S. presidents George Bush and Bill Clinton engaged in productive summit meetings with Russian president Boris Yeltsin. The United States and its allies gave billions of dollars in loans and assistance to Russia as the onetime center of world communism sought to reform itself into a capitalist democracy. The United States also provided assistance to Russia to help dismantle its nuclear weapons. The governments of the United States and Russia successfully negotiated and signed the START II (Strategic Arms Reductions Talks) agreement in 1993, which called for both countries to significantly reduce their nuclear weapons arsenals. The two countries agreed in 1994 to "de-target" their nuclear missiles aimed at each other. Russia lent its support to several U.S. initiatives, agreeing, for example, to participate in peacekeeping operations in Bosnia in 1995.

However, as the 1990s drew to a close the relationship between the two former rival superpowers became strained. Western aid to Russia has decreased as concerns have been raised over corruption and economic mismanagement. START III talks have been stalled by the refusal of the Russian Duma (parliament) to ratify the START II agreement. Russia has also voiced opposition to U.S. policy in Iraq and other parts of the world.

A central thorn in U.S.-Russian relations has been the status of the North Atlantic Treaty Organization (NATO), a military alliance created in 1949 linking the United States and Western Europe as common defenders against a possible Soviet Union attack. The collapse of the Soviet Union has caused some observers, both in Russia and the United States, to question whether NATO should continue to exist—and whether Russia should still be treated as a threat.

The viewpoints in the following chapter present several perspectives on NATO and on American foreign policy concerning Russia.

| "Our work with [Russia] has helped secure
| ... breakthroughs that are clearly in the
| national interest."

The United States Should Continue Its Strategic Partnership with Russia

Strobe Talbott

Strobe Talbott was appointed deputy secretary of state in 1994 by President Bill Clinton. A former *Time* magazine editor and author of several books on the Soviet Union, Talbott has been the leading architect of U.S. foreign policy toward Russia and other former Soviet states. In the following viewpoint, taken from testimony given before the Senate Foreign Relations Committee in September 1999, Talbott defends the Clinton administration's record on U.S.-Russian relations. He believes the United States should continue to engage Russia, encourage its leaders to undertake democratic and capitalist reforms, and cooperate with them in nuclear arms control and other issues. By improving relations with Russia, the United States has enhanced its own national security, he concludes.

As you read, consider the following questions:
1. What should be the fundamental test of America's Russian policy, according to Talbott?
2. What important breakthroughs in U.S.-Russian relations does Talbott identify?

Excerpted from Strobe Talbott, testimony before the Senate Foreign Relations Committee, September 23, 1999.

I welcome the opportunity to discuss with the [Senate Foreign Relations] Committee developments in Russia and U.S. policy toward that country. . . . Russia is much on our minds these days, and rightly so. Secretary Albright is at the United Nations this week [in September 1999], and she has heard repeatedly from our friends and allies around the world that Russia is much on their minds too. They are counting on us to manage U.S.-Russian relations with skill, foresight, and clarity of purpose.

Not for the first time and not for the last, the Russians are undergoing what many of them call "a time of troubles." Those troubles pose a complex set of challenges to American foreign and national security policy. The trouble that has received the most attention of late is a spate of allegations and revelations about large-scale financial malfeasance, including charges of money-laundering through American banks.

The challenge to us is threefold: first, to ensure that we are enforcing our own laws and protecting Americans from international organized crime; second, to ensure that we are doing everything we can to protect the integrity and effectiveness of our bilateral and international assistance programs; third, to intensify our supportive and cooperative work with those Russians who realize—as Foreign Minister [Igor] Ivanov stressed in New York when he met with Secretary [of State Madeleine K.] Albright on Monday and with President [Bill] Clinton yesterday [September 21 and 22, 1999]—that their country and their people are suffering from rampant crime and corruption and who are therefore committed to fighting back against that scourge.

Russia has other troubles too. Continued fighting between insurgents and Russian troops in the northern Caucasus is claiming hundreds of lives. Terrorist bombings in Moscow and two other cities have exceeded the death toll of Oklahoma City and the World Trade Center combined. Like crime and corruption, terrorism is not just a Russian problem—it's a global one, and like crime and corruption, it won't prove susceptible to just a Russian solution.

On both issues, the Government of Russia has sought help from us and from others. One of the several issues we in the Executive Branch are discussing in our current consultations with the Congress . . . is the terms of our ability to provide that help and the strategic goals that our support for Russian reform is meant to serve.

America's National Security

Let me, before going to your questions, suggest an overall context for that discussion: First and foremost, our policy must advance the national security interest of the United States—both in the short term and the long term. The test we must apply—day in and day out, year in and year out, from one Administration to the next—is whether the American people are safer as a result of our policy. This Administration's Russia policy meets that test.

When we came into office, there were roughly 10,000 intercontinental nuclear weapons in four states of the former Soviet Union; most were aimed at the United States. Today, there are about half as many—some 5,000; they're only in Russia, none are targeted at us, and we're discussing significant further reductions in overall numbers and further steps to diminish the nuclear threat in all its aspects.

That's one of several issues of vital importance to the U.S. that Secretary Albright and Minister Ivanov grappled with earlier this week, along with peace in the Middle East, in the Balkans, in the Gulf—and in the Caucasus. My point is simply this: Corruption is an important issue that we are taking very seriously. But as we probe its cause and as we refine our response, we must keep in mind that it is part of a much larger process underway in a vast and complex country—a country whose nature as a state and whose role in the world will have a lot to do with what sort of 21st century awaits us.

An Extraordinary Transformation

For a decade now, Russia has been undergoing an extraordinary transformation. In fact, it is undergoing three transformations in one: from a dictatorship to an open society; from a command economy to a market economy; and from a totalitarian empire and ideological rival toward becoming what many Russians call—and aspire to as—a "normal, modern state," integrated into the international community of which we are a part. We've been helping keep that process going.

Just as one example, the FREEDOM Support Act [a U.S. foreign aid program to Russia and other former Soviet states] and other programs have helped Russia make dramatic improvements in the protection of human rights and religious freedoms. All of us are realistic about the difficulties. Russia's transformation has encountered plenty of obstacles, none greater and more challenging than the crucial need to create the laws and institutions that are necessary to fighting crime and corruption in an open society and market economy.

Russia Is Not Ours to Lose

Russia is not a watch or a set of keys that can be misplaced. It is a nation of almost 150 million people that has, for more than three centuries, been among the world's major powers. The suggestion made by some that Russia is ours to lose is arrogant; the suggestion that Russia is lost is simply wrong.

After all, since the Cold War ended, first President Bush and then President Clinton have pursued two basic goals in our relations with Russia. The first is to increase the safety of the American people by working to reduce Cold War arsenals, stop proliferation, and create a stable and undivided Europe. The second is to support Russia's effort to transform its political, economic and social institutions at home. Neither of these goals has been fully achieved. But neither has been lost. Each remains a work in progress. We remain determined to work with Russia and our allies to accomplish each.

Address by Madeleine K. Albright before the Carnegie Endowment for International Peace, September 16, 1999.

Still, the transformation continues and so must our commitment to stay engaged. While there are no easy answers and no quick answers to what ails the Russian body politic today, there is one over-arching principle that is fundamental to creating the forces for change that will drive the scourge of corruption out of Russian society, and that is democracy. When I was in Moscow 2 weeks ago [in September 1999], I was struck, yet again, by the preoccupation of virtually everyone I met with the upcoming parliamentary and presidential elections. For the first time in their history, Russian citizens are now voters; they can register their grievances and express their aspirations through the ballot box—or, for that matter, on a soap box. Their grievances prominently include disgust with corruption; their aspirations prominently include good governance, honest governance.

If they and the leaders they choose can stay on the course of constitutional rule and electoral democracy, not only will Russia's own people be better off, but so will our own. That's the hard-headed essence of why we must continue to support them in coping with the difficulties they face, notably including those that are in the headlines today. That is also why Russia's current problems with crime and corruption are different from the corruption that was so entrenched in Soviet communism. Indeed, one way to look at today's troubles in Russia is as part of the legacy of an evil past and a result of an incomplete but ongoing transition to a better future. The solution to those troubles is for them to keep moving forward and for us to support them as they do so.

Since the Cold War ended, the United States has . . . pursued two basic goals in our relations with Russia. The first is to increase our security by reducing Cold War arsenals, stopping proliferation, and encouraging stability and integration in Europe. The second is to support Russia's effort to transform its political, economic, and social institutions. Both of these goals are very much works in progress.

Important Breakthroughs

In the years since Russia helped bring the Soviet system to an end, our work with that nation has helped secure some breakthroughs that are clearly in the national interest:

First, the Soviet Union dissolved in a largely peaceful fashion with its nuclear weapons in secure hands, an outcome that was not foreordained. Imagine the chaos the world would face if the Soviet Union and its nuclear arsenal had come apart in the same way Yugoslavia has. First the Bush Administration and then the Clinton Administration worked assiduously to ensure that such a nightmare did not come to pass.

Second, Russia helped dismantle the apparatus of the Soviet system and has rejected the forcible reformation of the Soviet Union or the creation of a new totalitarian superstate. It has no practical option to turn back the clock.

Third, the people of Russia and their leaders have embraced democracy and have held a series of free and fair elections at the national and local levels, followed by a stable transition of offices and power, and, more broadly, they are assembling the building blocks of a civil society based on public participation.

Fourth, Russia has made important strides in replacing central planning with the infrastructure and institutions of a market economy.

Fifth, and equally important, Russia remains committed to working as constructively as possible with the U.S. and other nations of the international community.

International support is an essential part of helping Russia take difficult internal steps to restructure itself.

The President, the Vice President [Al Gore], Secretary Albright, and the rest of us have always understood that in transforming itself, Russia has been tearing down dysfunctional Soviet structures, but it has only begun to put in place the mechanisms of a modern state.

An Enormous Task

This is an enormous and time-consuming task. Russia, after a millennium of autocracy and more than 70 years of communism, had little or no historical memory of civil society, of a market economy, or of the rule of law. The Soviet system itself was in many ways institutionalized criminality. I first heard the phrase "kleptocracy" used to describe the Soviet state. There are no "good old days" of real law and order or legitimate private enterprise to which Russia can return.

In short, crime and corruption are part of the grim legacy of the Soviet communist experience. The rampancy of that problem has impeded Russia's own progress and impeded our ability to help Russia move forward. Moreover, as Russia dismantled communism and sought to create a new market economy, the weaknesses inherent in its new economic institutions created vulnerabilities to corruption. That is why, in his 1995 visit to Moscow, President Clinton called for "a market based on law, not lawlessness."

Yet, just as we cited these dangers, we were also engaged in finding solutions. U.S. assistance, as well as that of multilateral bodies such as the International Monetary Fund (IMF), have focused on building the broader structures that will allow the democratic citizens of Russia—who have the most to lose from corruption—to bring transparency and accountability to both government and business dealings.

We have consistently emphasized the need for transparency and accountability in our dealings with Russia and in the dealings of the international financial institutions working with Russia. When problems have arisen, we have insisted on full and complete investigations and will continue to do so. In instances where there have been concerns about Russian practices, the IMF has tightened controls, performed audits, and reduced lending levels. . . .

Supporting Grassroots Change

I have referred several times to the sheer size of Russia. In that connection, I would like to emphasize that three-quarters of FREEDOM Support Act assistance is spent on programs that do not involve the Russian Government, as part of our effort to help build grassroots support for change. The U.S. government has worked to build relationships with Russian law enforcement and judicial entities and to help them increase their capabilities to operate in a professional and ethical manner. We have also promoted the rule of law at the grassroots level by working with non-governmental organizations, human rights advocates, and independent media watchdogs, as well as by promoting ethical business practices. . . .

Law enforcement agreements with Russia allow us to share information on cases and cooperate on the investigation, prosecution, and prevention of crime. The current Mutual Legal Assistance Agreement between the United States and Russia allows each side to request information, interviews, and other background material to support investigations. In June 1999, the U.S. and Russia signed a Mutual Legal Assistance Treaty which, when ratified and brought into force, will replace the Agreement. The Treaty will expand and strengthen the scope of cooperation, facilitating investigation and prosecution of transnational criminals. . . .

In conclusion, Mr. Chairman, Secretary Albright has asked

me to use this occasion to reiterate the case that she has made to you and your colleagues for the resources we need in order to defend and advance American interests. Congress is currently proposing a cut of between 25–30% from the President's FREEDOM Support Act budget request for programs in Russia and elsewhere in the New Independent States. The Secretary believes such cuts would be dangerously short-sighted because the purposes of this assistance—from building an independent media to promoting small businesses—are fundamentally in our interests. She hopes that engagement with Russia would be something Republicans and Democrats can agree on. Engagement is a bipartisan foreign goal because it serves the long-term interests of the American people.

"The results of Clinton's policy have been disastrous. The Russian breakthrough has turned into a breakdown."

The United States Should Not Continue Its Strategic Partnership with Russia

Jacob Heilbrun

American policy toward Russia in the 1990s has been marked by unwavering support of Russian president Boris Yeltsin, argues Jacob Heilbrun in the following viewpoint, and has failed dismally to achieve its ambitious objective of turning Russia into a cooperative partner. Billions of dollars of U.S. monetary aid to Russia have been lost to corruption, he asserts, while an anti-American backlash has risen among Russia's people, who associate the United States with the unpopular Yeltsin regime. In addition, Russia has pursued several foreign policy initiatives that run counter to U.S. interests. Heilbrun recommends that the United States give up all pretense of a strategic partnership with the Russian Federation and withhold foreign assistance unless Russia undergoes genuine democratic reforms. America might even need to prepare for the possibility of Russia's eventual dissolution. Heilbrun is a senior editor for the *New Republic* magazine.

As you read, consider the following questions:
1. How does Heilbrun characterize Russian reformers such as Anatoly Chubais?
2. What fundamental fact about Russia must U.S. foreign policy leaders, according to Heilbrun?

In July 1998, Vice President Al Gore and then-Russian Prime Minister Sergei Kiriyenko met in Moscow to announce an ambitious joint program they called the nuclear cities initiative. The initiative, they explained, would create research jobs for weapons scientists in the ten "closed cities" that constitute Russia's nuclear weapons complex, thus ensuring that the scientists wouldn't work on developing new weapons of mass destruction—for Russia or for rogue nations. Gore was elated. "It is simultaneously visionary and pragmatic," he said, "to join hands in reaching those objectives."

But, eight months later, those objectives seem as remote as ever. According to a lengthy study released by the General Accounting Office in February [1999], many of the hundreds of Russian nuclear disarmament projects funded by the Department of Energy have gone badly awry. More than half the money has stayed in the United States, some of it has further subsidized scientists working on weapons of mass destruction, and it's not clear how much money scientists have actually received (Russian nuclear institutes use the subsidies to pay taxes to Moscow). The study concludes: "Some 'dual-use' projects may have unintentionally provided defense-related information—an outcome that could negatively affect U.S. national security interests."

This is not exactly shocking news. Every day seems to bring fresh revelations about how the Russian government has squandered or stolen the billions of dollars that the United States, Europe, the World Bank, and the International Monetary Fund have pumped into the country—while a few Russian oligarchs get richer and richer. . . .

The Clinton Administration's Russia Policy

If news of Russian waste, fraud, and abuse has become predictable, so has the Clinton administration's response. Though he's already dealing with his third Russian prime minister, Gore is set to meet with Yevgeny Primakov at the end of March [1999]—to continue the work of his special high-level commission begun with then-Prime Minister Viktor Chernomyrdin to establish cooperation on nuclear and environmental problems. As for the president himself, a national security official says he "has been dogged in a way you can't see on other foreign policy issues. However much bad news there is, he sees Russia as a country politically making a positive contribution."

The administration's reluctance to change policy is not surprising. Policy shifts are always painful—it took several years for the Truman administration to adjust to the Communist threat—and creating a new Russia from the detritus left behind by seven decades of communism was bound to be a daunting task. The payoff looked to be great: turning Russia, a historic foe, into a cooperative partner, thereby ensuring European security and a new market for American goods. Coupled with fears of the selling-off of the Russian nuclear force to terrorists and dictators, the administration could, and did, plausibly argue that it was following the only sensible course. The administration's optimism about where things were headed was captured by Deputy Secretary of State Strobe Talbott when he declared in August 1997 that Russia was becoming a "normal, modern state. . . . It may be on the brink of a breakthrough."

But the Russian financial collapse last August [1998] suggests that, however laudable the intentions, the results of Clinton's policy have been disastrous. The Russian breakthrough has turned into a breakdown. Indeed, the American attempt to buy Russian goodwill has boomeranged: it simply associated the United States with a regime that is widely (and correctly) viewed by ordinary Russians as erratic, authoritarian, and corrupt. This, in turn, has fueled a nationalistic, anti-American backlash. And the Kremlin, desperate to preserve the fiction that Russia is still a "great power" like the United States, pockets American subventions and then seeks to complicate and subvert our foreign policy whenever and wherever it can.

The architect of administration policy has been Strobe Talbott. Just as Talbott's view of the cold war was typified by hand-wringing about America's culpability for frightening the Soviet Union, so he views the U.S. today as needing to allay Russian fears of "encirclement." "Suspicions of each other's motives," said Talbott in 1996, "could prove self-justifying, and pessimistic prophecies about the future of the relationship may be self-fulfilling. . . . We saw enough of this kind of vicious cycle during the cold war."

To avoid this "cycle," the administration immediately began to arrange loan agreements with the Kremlin. Thus Clinton's first foreign trip as president was to Vancouver in April 1993, where he met with Boris Yeltsin and sealed the U.S.-Russian "new democratic partnership" with a promised $1.6 billion in aid. As George Washington University Professor Janine R. Wedel shows in *Collision and Collusion*, the administration singled out a group of self-styled reformers known in Russia as the "Chubais clan"—after St. Petersburg politician Anatoly Chubais—and funneled hundreds of millions of dollars through it into the Russian economy. The contacts between these reformers and the Clinton administration could not have been closer. Lawrence Summers, deputy secretary of the U.S. Treasury, worked to help propel them into government—and, through them, to guide Russian economic policy.

Reformers Line Their Own Pockets

The Clinton administration assumed that the Russian reformers were actually interested in reform. But they weren't. What they were interested in was lining their own pockets. The Chubais clique—which Summers had called a "dream team"—turned out to be a nightmare. For example, when Chubais oversaw the sale of Russia's vast factories and firms, Russia's banks were allowed to run the auctions and participate in them—while barring foreigners from bidding altogether. With the field thus rigged, oligarchs like Chernomyrdin were able to snap up the companies at bargain-basement prices. Five percent of Lukoil, Russia's biggest oil company, was sold for $250 million—just a little more than the minimum reserve bid. Bank Imperil, part of Chernomyrdin's Gazprom, Russia's natural gas monopoly, was the beneficiary. (In 1997, Izvestia showed that a think tank established by Chubais had taken a $3 million interest-free loan from the Stolichny Bank, then placed the money in an investment fund run by one of Chubais's friends. Chubais brazenly responded that "an interest-free loan . . . is absolutely normal . . . in both Russia and any other democratic country.")

Of course, the Chubais clan was not just duping Russians.

They fooled the West, too—as the International Monetary Fund eventually learned. The IMF had been supplying a steady infusion of funds to the Yeltsin government; Russia's outstanding debt to the IMF in 1998 was $2.8 billion. U.S. pressure helped prompt the IMF to keep lending, problems with the Russian government's behavior notwithstanding. In 1996, for instance, it was clear that the IMF's loans were, in effect, subsidizing the bloody Russian crackdown in Chechnya. IMF Managing Director Michel Camdessus said, "Are we financing Chechnya? . . . Those who tell me, 'You are financing Chechnya,' in some ways, yes, as we finance Russia." In September 1998, Chubais told the Moscow newspaper *Kommersant* that Russia "conned" the IMF and Western leaders out of a $20 billion bailout package the previous July by deceiving them about the state of the Russian economy. Had they told the truth, the IMF and other institutions, said Chubais, "would have stopped dealing with us forever."

Warnings have been aired for some time now, as they were in February [1999], at a conference on Russian civil society at the Library of Congress sponsored by the Templeton Foundation. There, Father Georgi Edelshtein, a former Soviet dissident, lamented, "We haven't seen a dollar, not a single kopeck." He added: "When you Americans come . . . to distribute aid personally we see it. Otherwise, nothing. Don't you worry, they'll steal it."

But the fundamentals of the administration's policy have not adjusted accordingly. When Yeltsin peremptorily sacked Chernomyrdin, Gore visited Moscow to hail Sergei Kiriyenko, Chernomyrdin's successor. Kiriyenko, Gore said, had "a very impressive understanding of economic reform and what must be done in order to advance reform." But there was no way of knowing whether Kiriyenko would in fact pursue reform—he was a 35-year-old energy minister promoted overnight to prime minister. A few months later, he was sacked. As Dimitri K. Simes cogently observes in the Winter 1998/99 *National Interest*: "The fulsome praise for the new Russian government seemed to reflect the Clinton administration's predisposition to find something positive in almost any move taken by Yeltsin. . . . The near euphoria in Washington was, however, totally divorced from realities in Russia."

And so it remains. The Republican Congress has tried to put the brakes on aid, but Clinton has called for $200 million in new assistance this year [1999]. In addition, the administration continues to back a $660 million package for Russia's space program, while World Bank loans—largely funded by American taxpayers—may come to another $6 billion in the next year and a half. (That's in addition to the $11.4 billion the bank has already loaned the Russians.) . . .

KLEPTOCRACY

LOANS

HOW
NEW RUSSIA
WORKS

As if the sheer waste of money were not bad enough, there's another troubling consequence of the Clinton administration's strategic partnership with Russia—the fact that it's undercutting other elements of U.S. foreign policy. There is an intimate link between the Russian economy and its posture abroad. Put simply, the worse things get at home, the more hostile Russia gets in foreign affairs. The United States has spared no effort to cater to Russian concerns—particularly when it comes to condoning the Russian massacres in Chechnya. NATO expansion was handled with kid gloves, to the point of giving the Russians a representative at NATO. Some will say that Russian assertiveness is a result of NATO expansion, but the issue is dead in Russia. The fact remains that Russia has rewarded American understanding with truculence and challenges to what Primakov has called a "unipolar" American world.

Russia's Truculence

Consider Russia's recent actions in the Middle East. In 1991, Russia was an active supporter of U.S. policy there. It backed the Arab-Israeli peace process as well as sanctions against Libya; during the Persian Gulf crisis, it sent two warships to bolster sanctions against Iraq. Yet, by the mid-'90s, Yeltsin—responding to pressure from the Duma—was reestablishing relations with U.S. foes in the region. First the Russians and Iraqis set up regular visits between their diplomats; then, in 1994, the Russians stepped up arms sales to Iran. A year later, and despite strong U.S. opposition, Russia began selling nuclear technology to Iran.

In 1997, Yeltsin welcomed Ali Akbar Nateq-Nouri, the Iranian speaker of the parliament, to Russia on an official visit. "We have good, positive cooperation with Iran, which shows a tendency to grow," the Russian president said. The shift in the Russian attitude toward the Middle East was signaled earlier when Yeltsin fired the liberal, pro-Western Foreign Minister Andrei Kozyrev in 1996—and replaced him with Primakov. Primakov visited Tehran in December 1996 to improve relations; in November, Russia had announced that it would sell to Iran $4 billion in military equipment over the next ten years, though Gore had made efforts to curb the sales.

The Iranians had done their part to court favor with the Russians. Specifically, they had avoided promoting Islamist sentiments in the former Soviet Central Asian republics. But forging an alliance with Iran also appealed to the Russians because it afforded an opportunity to contain American influence in the region. As the newspaper *Segodnea* explained: "NATO's expansion eastward is making Russia look around hurriedly for at least some kind of strategic allies. In this situation, the anti-Western and anti-American regime in Iran would be a natural and very important partner."

What practical implications has Russian support for Iran had? Last July [1998], Tehran successfully conducted the first flight test of the medium-range ballistic missile Shahab-3, which can reach targets up to 1,500 kilometers away. Testifying before the Senate on February 2 [1999], Director of Central Intelligence George Tenet noted that "expertise and materiel from Russia has continued to assist the Iranian missile . . . effort. This assistance is continuing as we speak, and there is no doubt that it will play a crucial role in Iran's ability to develop more sophisticated and longer-range missiles." Nevertheless, the Clinton administration continues to press its agenda gingerly. As one administration official puts it, "For the past eighteen months, we've moved on the issue to show Russians that they are selling out their national interests" because Iran is a neighbor of Russia and could target it. But "the Russians are now in a stonewalling mode." In an October [1998] speech, State Department official Stephen Sestanovich declared: "We have been completely candid with the Russians about our view of Iran, but we have not expected to be able to persuade them to adopt our policy on Iran in particular. We have not really tried to do so. We have tried, instead, to build on a higher realism—on a recognition of the threat that the flow of technology to Iran's nuclear and ballistic missile programs poses to Russia itself—and to Russian-America cooperation."

Russia's dalliance with Iraq is another case study in our strategic partner acting in a very unpartnerly way. Primakov, a comrade of [Iraq dictator] Saddam Hussein's from the days when Primakov was working for the KGB in the Middle East, has made no secret of his wish to cultivate relations with Iraq. Russia has become Iraq's staunchest backer in the U.N. Security Council; when the United States finally launched a four-day air strike against Iraq in mid-December, Russia's ambassador to the U.N. complained about "gross violations of the rule of law." Yeltsin, from his sickbed, expressed "the most serious concern, a feeling of dismay and deep alarm." But Yeltsin is opposed to the U.S. use of force anywhere: when the United States launched cruise missiles in the Sudan and Afghanistan in retaliation for terrorism, Yeltsin declared, "I am outraged and condemn this."

Russia's behavior has been similarly obstreperous in the Balkans. With regard to the Serb campaign to dominate

Kosovo, Foreign Minister Ivanov declared in September [1998] that "The use of force, whether by NATO or any other power, will lead to even more serious consequences." The Balkans, said Ivanov, "have always been a zone of special strategic interest for Russia." In October, after diplomat Richard Holbrooke ended his talks in Belgrade by issuing an ultimatum to the Serbs, Russia recalled its ambassador and military representative from NATO. General Leonid Ivashov, head of the chief administration for international military cooperation, said that a NATO bombing would allow Russia to start full-scale military cooperation with Belgrade. In Ivashov's words, "If NATO takes action in Kosovo, Russia will regard it as an act of aggression against Yugoslavia. . . . The alliance's armed forces have projected a similar scenario to Russia as well; NATO's next targets could be other countries of Europe and the Commonwealth of Independent States."

The Kremlin ultimately disavowed Ivashov's remarks, but they point to the hostility that the Russian military establishment feels toward the United States. . . .

An Alternative Policy

The standard administration response to criticism of its Russia policy is, What's the alternative? But, while the concerns about antagonizing a nation beset by unrest, on the verge of economic collapse, and with a nuclear capability are legitimate, there is in fact another policy. And that policy must begin with the recognition that Russia is not a second- or even a third-rate power—it's powerless.

For one thing, Russia's economic debility means that it may soon be incapable of fielding a credible nuclear threat. So many of its nuclear submarines have been decommissioned that, according to Barry Renfrew of the Associated Press, only three are thought to be on patrol at any one time. The air force's Bear bombers are more than 40 years old; pilots only get a few hours of flying time a year. Many land-based missiles have outlived their natural life span, and, while new missile plans are under way, Russia is unable to fund them.

Given Russian decrepitude, perhaps the Clinton administration should be less hesitant about standing up to Moscow. When the Russians use the U.N. Security Council to thwart U.S. policy, the United States could threaten to sever assistance packages. In addition, the United States ought to move ahead with research on its own anti-ballistic missile defense program. . . . The United States will have to renegotiate the ABM Treaty, negotiated with the now defunct Soviet Union, or, if Russia refuses, even consider abrogating it. The threat of a missile launch against Japan by North Korea makes a local theater missile defense system of not inconsiderable importance.

But perhaps the most important step of all would be to recognize that the United States is incapable of propping up the Russian Federation. Primakov himself warned in late February 1999 that the Kremlin's control over Russia is "not a solid line" but "a vertical line—broken." (Primakov has suggested that Russia should end the popular election of governors and instead have them report directly to the Kremlin, as was the case during the Soviet era.) During the August 1998 crisis, regional leaders asserted control over trade and tax policy. In Vladivostok, for example, the Maritime Territory Council of Chief Administrators met to pass price controls on gasoline, detergents, and other items. In Kirov, Governor Vladimir Sergeyenkov sought to reestablish a state monopoly over the alcohol industry. Most of the countries that form the Commonwealth of Independent States are also trying to pull away from Russia—including Ukraine and Kazakhstan, which make up much of Russia's trade with the CIS. A *Kommersant* article observed, "Not only has the Russian crisis driven the national economy to the brink of disaster, it has utterly undermined confidence in Russia as an integrating center and jeopardized the very existence of the CIS in its current form."

Yes, the breakup of the Russian Federation could be the horror scenario that doomsayers predict—massive immigration out of the country, civil war, and the spread of loose nukes. But that outcome is not inevitable. Were devolution to take place—say, a Siberian republic, a St. Petersburg city-state, and so on—Russians might be able to tackle their economic problems at the local level. As it stands, they are heavily penalized by Moscow, which strips them of precious resources and imposes, or seeks to impose, onerous taxes. The provinces have seen little Western aid because it has stayed in Moscow, lining the pockets of American consultants and the various economic clans that have sprung up since 1991.

Certainly, it would be foolhardy for the United States to foment the breakup of Russia. Already, nationalists claim that this is in fact official American policy. But it would be prudent for the United States to prepare for Russia's dissolution by, say, stepping up aid to the states on its periphery, most notably Ukraine.

A Turbulent Relationship Is Unavoidable

In any case, a more turbulent relationship with Russia is unavoidable. Now that the Communists in the Duma are calling for a return to a Soviet-style constitution and the renationalization of businesses in return for permitting Primakov to stay in power, preserving a strategic partnership will be harder than ever. None of the likely contenders for the Russian presidency in 2000, from Moscow Mayor Yuri Luzhkov to Primakov, would take a friendly position toward the United States.

When Gore meets with Primakov in March [1999], he should insist that Russia undertake real economic reform or get along without more Western money. But taking a tougher line on Russia would fly in the face of what much of the foreign policy establishment still recommends. In the *New York Times* on February 16 [1999], for example, [columnist] Thomas Friedman wrote: "The West right now should focus on organizing forgiveness and a restructuring of Russia's debts, to take the pressure off the Yevgeny Primakov Government, so it can run a credible budget that might begin to draw back some private investment, stop the bleeding, and provide a reasonably stable environment for the December Duma elections." This amounts to the Talbottian formula already applied to the ailing Russian state: give, give, give. But isn't it time to ask what America is getting in return?

"*NATO expansion poisons the well in U.S.-Russian relations.*"

NATO Enlargement Endangers U.S.-Russian Relations

Gary Hart and Gordon Humphrey

The North Atlantic Treaty Organization (NATO) was formed in 1949 by the United States and several European nations. For the next four decades, Europe was divided between NATO and the Warsaw Pact, the military alliance between the Soviet Union and Eastern Europe. NATO remained an integral part of European and American foreign policy even after the end of the Cold War and the disbanding of the Warsaw Pact in 1991. In April 1998 Congress debated whether to ratify the admission of three former Warsaw Pact members—Poland, Hungary, and the Czech Republic—into NATO. In the following viewpoint, Gary Hart and Gordon Humphrey argue that taking this step would needlessly antagonize Russian leaders. The United States should instead work to improve and maintain friendly relations with Russia and to reduce Russia's arsenal of nuclear weapons, the authors conclude. Hart and Humphrey are both former U.S. senators, representing Colorado and New Hampshire respectively. Congress did vote to approve of NATO enlargement on April 30, 1998; the countries formally entered NATO in March 1999.

As you read, consider the following questions:

1. Why do the authors believe that NATO expansion is unnecessary?
2. How do the authors respond to the argument that ordinary Russians do not care about NATO expansion?

Reprinted from Gary Hart and Gordon Humphrey, "Creating a Cold Peace by Expanding NATO," *Cato This Just In*, March 20, 1998. Reprinted with permission from The Cato Institute; www.cato.org.

The U.S. Senate will soon cast a vote that will set the tone of U.S.-Russian relations for the next generation. If senators approve NATO membership for Poland, Hungary and the Czech Republic, NATO will move right up to Russia's border, seriously endangering the once-in-a-century opportunity for the United States to build a constructive relationship with that vast and important country. Russia is particularly sensitive about her province of Kaliningrad, which shares 432 kilometers of border with Poland.

Approval of Poland's application means NATO on Russia's border in 1999. If the Senate approves the first group of applicants, it can hardly deny membership to the next round of applicants, including Latvia, Lithuania and Estonia. Those nations share an additional 734 kilometers of border with Russia. Thus, the United States will have responded to the peaceful dissolution of the Soviet empire with an in-your-face deployment of the NATO alliance right on Russia's doorstep. Humiliating a former adversary is a dangerous thing for a great power to do, and we may pay dearly for our arrogance.

No Need for Expansion

There is simply no need to expand NATO. Even the proponents admit Russia poses no threat to her neighbors, nor could she for many years to come even under the worst of circumstances. Eastern and Central Europe do not need a military alliance, they need access to Western markets. Then why are supporters pushing NATO expansion? It got started in 1996 as an election-year ploy to pander to American voters who identify with the candidate nations. It has been carried forward on the argument that expanding NATO into Central and Eastern Europe promotes stability. Everyone is for stability. But how do we promote stability anywhere in Europe by promoting instability everywhere in Russia? Our highest priority ought to be the reduction of Russia's arsenal of nuclear weapons, which still constitutes a real and present threat to the United States. Resentment of NATO expansion prompted the Russian legislature to delay ratification of the START II Treaty that would shrink Russian and U.S. arsenals by 3,500 strategic nuclear missiles each. The refusal to

A Russian Reformer's Views on NATO Expansion

A Western-style democracy in Russia would be a partner with the West in confronting the challenges of the 21st century. Russia and the West would work together better to maintain control over weapons of mass destruction and would be more likely to cooperate in containing regional conflict in explosive areas like the Caucasus and Middle East. Finally, the rule of law would govern business relations and allow for economic development and growth beneficial for both societies. . . .

Russia's choice [to embrace or reject democracy] will be heavily influenced by the West. Unfortunately, up to this point, the West has not always promoted the correct path. Nowhere is this more evident than in the debate over NATO expansion. If a military alliance moves closer to a country's borders without incorporating that country, it means that the country's foreign policy has dismally failed. Talk that this is a different NATO, a NATO that is no longer a military alliance, is ridiculous. It is like saying that the hulking thing advancing toward your garden is not a tank because it is painted pink, carries flowers, and plays cheerful music. It does not matter how you dress it up; a pink tank is still a tank.

The most important message of NATO expansion for Russians, however, is that the political leaders of Western Europe and the United States do not believe that Russia can become a real Western-style democracy within the next decade or so. In their eyes, Russia, because of its history, is a second-class democracy. Perhaps this is understandable. The combination of Chechnya (an arbitrary war in which Russia unnecessarily killed 100,000 people), the collapse of the Russian army, failed economic reforms, a semi-criminal government, and Yeltsin's unpredictability has given the West enough justification to conclude that Russia, for the time being, cannot be a dependable partner and that NATO expansion should therefore continue.

Ironically, if the United States explained its push for NATO expansion in these terms to the Russian people, they would at least understand why the alliance is expanding and respect the West for its honesty. But when the West says to Russians: "Russian democracy is fine, Russian markets are fine, Russia's relationship with the West is fine, and therefore NATO is expanding to Russia's borders," the logic does not work, leaving the Russian people and their leaders bewildered and bitter. This resentment will only be exacerbated if the West continues its two-faced policy.

Grigory Yavlinsky, *Foreign Affairs*, May/June 1998.

ratify that important treaty, despite pleas from Presidents Clinton and Yeltsin, is a concrete example of the way NATO expansion strengthens the hands of the irresponsible elements at the expense of Russian reformers.

Further, NATO's encampment right on Russia's borders forces Moscow to rely more heavily on her large stockpile of tactical nuclear weapons left over from Soviet days. Moscow has lately renounced a no-first-strike policy. Given the decrepit state of Russia's conventional forces, she has little choice but to make do. Unfortunately, tactical nuclear weapons can be used to make up for inadequate conventional forces. How does forcing Russia to turn increasingly to tactical nuclear weapons promote stability?

Russia has an ugly nuclear mess on her hands. Forty thousand nuclear warheads and tons of nuclear weapons materials are scattered across her vast territories. Some are at risk of transfer to terrorists and rogue nations. Former ambassador to Russia Jack Matlock testified to the Senate Foreign Relations Committee, "When the people guarding [nuclear materials] have not been paid in six months . . . it is totally unreasonable to expect that all are going to resist the temptation of selling dangerous materials." Clearly, the United States should go all out to help Russia dismantle her excess nuclear warheads and to bring all warhead materials under strict controls. NATO expansion thwarts that effort, too.

Poisoning U.S.-Russian Relations

More broadly, NATO expansion poisons the well in U.S.-Russian relations. To contain Soviet communism, we fought two hot wars and a long cold war and spent perhaps $20 trillion. For 45 years, our citizens bore a heavy burden, including the risk of nuclear war or nuclear accident. At last we have an opportunity to build friendly relations with Russia. NATO expansion puts that priceless opportunity at peril, risking the waste of an enormous sacrifice of American blood and treasure. Worse, it risks a resumption of a dangerous confrontation between the United States and Russia, two nations that ought to be friends.

Russian reformers who expected to be treated as friends and equals now find themselves cast beyond the pale as unworthy, uncivilized and unwashed. Russian leaders from across the entire spectrum bitterly resent NATO expansion. To dismiss their concern by saying ordinary Russians don't care misses the point. Ordinary Russians haven't the luxury of looking beyond the daily struggle to put food in front of their children. But Russians who make foreign policy care greatly, and they shape history. Proponents of expansion who say the Russians will "have to get over it" reveal an arrogance and a short-sightedness that serve us ill. NATO expansion may prove to be the most damaging mistake in international relations since the humiliation of Germany after World War I, an act of hubris most historians count as the cause of World War II.

4

"*Fears that the enlargement of the North Atlantic Treaty Organization . . . will disrupt ties between the United States and Russia are unfounded.*"

NATO Enlargement Does Not Endanger U.S.-Russian Relations

Ariel Cohen

In 1998 Congress debated whether to ratify the addition of three former Soviet allies—Poland, Hungary, and the Czech Republic—to the North Atlantic Treaty Organization (NATO). The countries were finally admitted to NATO, but some critics argued that this step would be a serious blunder that would antagonize Russia. In the following viewpoint, Ariel Cohen argues that those who fear that NATO enlargement would harm relations between the United States and Russia are mistaken. He argues that Russia is too dependent on investment and cooperation from the United States and Western Europe to embark on an anti-American foreign policy regardless of NATO's expansion. Cohen is a senior policy analyst for the Heritage Foundation, a conservative think tank.

As you read, consider the following questions:
1. Who opposes NATO in Russia, according to Cohen?
2. What real security threats does Russia face, according to the author?
3. What two objectives does Cohen insist that the United States and other Western nations pursue?

Reprinted from Ariel Cohen, "NATO Enlargement Is No Threat to U.S.-Russian Relations," *The Heritage Foundation Executive Memorandum*, no. 510, February 26, 1998. Reprinted with permission.

Fears that the enlargement of the North Atlantic Treaty Organization (NATO) to include Poland, Hungary, and the Czech Republic will disrupt ties between the United States and Russia are unfounded. Russia needs Western investment, technology, and cooperation to integrate into the global economy. In addition, the Western media overemphasize anti-NATO sentiment among Russians. Polls show that Russians worry more about payments of chronically delayed wages, low living standards, crime, and corruption. Russia's real security concerns, moreover, are with its Islamic neighbors and the People's Republic of China, not with the democratic West. Finally, even the Yeltsin administration, which vehemently opposes NATO enlargement, admits that the major threats to Russia are domestic, and that no foreign country currently endangers Russia's security.

Investment to Modernize Russia

Russia needs Western investment and technology to modernize its economy and society. A vitriolic anti-American campaign and an offensive military posture hinting at a new Cold War will scare off foreign investors and might jeopardize multilateral economic assistance. Russia will not risk access to the benefits the West can offer just to derail Polish, Czech, and Hungarian membership in NATO. Russian reformers understand that enhanced stability and democracy in Central and Eastern Europe are in Russia's interests.

Russian reformers also understand that Russia can benefit from cooperation with NATO on such issues as civil-military relations, fighting crime and corruption in the military, protecting the rights of enlisted personnel, and cutting the military budget and manpower. NATO has expertise in these areas that it will share willingly with Russia.

The Battle Within

Strong opposition to NATO expansion comes from the Russian foreign policy and security elite, a group composed almost entirely of Soviet-vintage Cold Warriors. Anti-Western leftists, imperialists, and nationalists—the so-called Eurasianists—see Russia as a unique imperial entity spanning Europe and Asia, dominating its former vassals and opposing the United States, possibly in an alliance with China and Iran. They have attempted to use the NATO enlargement debate to draw Russia away from the West. If NATO expands to the east, Eurasianists fear the imperial option of Russia's renewed domination in Eastern and Central Europe could be foreclosed forever.

Such democrats as former acting prime minister Yegor Gaidar, however, and even the populist-nationalist General Alexander Lebed have asserted that NATO enlargement is the business of NATO (and the new members), and that Russia has nothing to fear of the West. Reformers eventually would like to see Russia as a part of the West, and possibly, a partner in NATO.

A positive step toward this goal was taken in the Founding Act on Relations between Russia and NATO signed in Paris on May 27, 1997. In that document, Russia and NATO created a bilateral council and permanent missions that are now working in Moscow and Brussels. The council gives Russia an opportunity to be part of all discussions on issues of mutual interest, and gives Russia a voice, but not a veto, in NATO decisions. This arrangement will make Russia a genuine part of the European security equation.

The Average Russian Does Not Care

The battles of the policy elites have had little effect on the average Russian. The general public paid little attention to the NATO debate, rightly considering it an "inside-the-Moscow-Beltway" issue. United States Information Agency (USIA) polls conducted in October 1996 and April 1997 showed 78 percent of the broad public knew little or nothing about the pending enlargement. Of those polled, less than 40 percent opposed enlargement, placing concerns over wages, the economy, crime, and corruption far above foreign policy and defense issues. And 70 percent of the Russians polled also indicated their belief that the special relationship with NATO would be in Russia's interests.

No Real Threat

Some Russians oppose NATO enlargement because they are reminded of the long history of invasions from the West. They fear that the move eastward might be the prelude to another attack. Gennady Zyuganov (leader of the Communist Party of Russia, which boasts the largest faction in the State Duma) repeatedly has compared the pending NATO enlargement with the eve of the Nazi invasion in 1941. Ultra-nationalist Vladimir Zhirinovsky often invokes the specter of a U.S. attack on Russia.

The comparison with the Nazis, of course, is ludicrous. NATO has no expansionist designs on Russia; as a defensive alliance, it has no capability to achieve them. In addition, there is no common border between Russia proper and the new members (except for the small enclave of Kaliningrad—known as Koenigsberg before 1945—locked between Poland and Lithuania) from which to launch an attack.

Moreover, the Yeltsin administration's official national security doctrine, which was published in December 1997, clearly states that foreign countries currently do not pose a threat to Russia's security. Crime, corruption, a poorly managed economy, poverty, and social malaise are the real dangers.

Complementary Objectives

Many reject NATO enlargement out of a desire to preserve a Russian sphere of influence. If Russia cannot accept the legitimate rights of its neighbors to choose their security arrangements, a policy they embraced in the NATO-Russia Founding Act, then NATO's role in Europe will prove even more important.

NATO enlargement and deeper NATO-Russian relations both have immense value for the United States and Europe if they are pursued properly. They are complementary and reinforcing objectives. The best outcome for the United States and Europe is for both tracks to succeed. A zero-sum debate about them, therefore, misses the point.

Richard Lugar, *Roll Call*, March 9, 1998.

Most Russians, too, understand that their most significant security challenges today lie elsewhere. For example, China is pouring half a million immigrants a year into the largely empty Russian land between Lake Baikal in Siberia and the Pacific Ocean. Chinese economic and technological growth has outstripped Russia's by far. Friction with Islamic neighbors in the northern Caucasus, such as the Chechens and possibly others in the future, and bloody entanglements in faraway places like Tajikistan demonstrate where the real threats are. With conflicts possible to the south and east, Russia should be interested in securing its western borders by having democratic neighbors—and especially Germany, which twice in this century sparked world wars—in a stable, democratic alliance.

What the West Can Do

Eventually bringing Russia into the Western orbit will benefit both Russia and the United States. Post-communist Russia needs to be engaged—not isolated—on the global scene, including on issues of European security. Russian objections to the current round of NATO enlargement are not widespread popular sentiments but rather a facet of Moscow's political games. The United States should mount a comprehensive program, using the United States Information Agency (USIA) and other avenues of public diplomacy, to explain the truth about NATO enlargement to Russia's media and general public. Once the facts are known, Russians will understand that the ascendancy of the new members into the alliance in no way prevents the United States from continuing to work with Russia to enhance bilateral and multilateral security cooperation.

"Barring the collapse of the reform process, 2010 would seem a reasonable target date for Russia's entry into NATO."

NATO Enlargement Should Eventually Incorporate Russia

Charles A. Kupchan

In April 1998 Congress voted to approve the inclusion of three countries—Poland, Hungary, and the Czech Republic—into the North Atlantic Treaty Organization (NATO), the U.S.-led military alliance whose purpose for many years was to defend Western Europe against a possible invasion by the Soviet Union. The demise of the Soviet Union has led to much debate on NATO's future. In the following viewpoint, Charles A. Kupchan argues that Russia should be the next country admitted into NATO. Russia will be thereby peacefully involved in Europe's affairs, he contends, and democratic reform will be encouraged within Russia. Kupchan is a professor at Georgetown University and a senior fellow at the Council on Foreign Relations.

As you read, consider the following questions:

1. What three reasons does Kupchan give for including Russia within NATO?
2. What three reasons does the author provide for his optimism about Russia's future?
3. Why, in the author's view, should Russia no longer be considered an adversary of the West?

Excerpted from Charles A. Kupchan, "Rethinking Europe," *The National Interest*, Summer 1999. Copyright © *The National Interest*, no. 56, Washington, D.C. Reprinted with permission.

NATO should never have embarked on enlargement into Central Europe; the costs plainly outweigh the benefits. But now that enlargement has begun, sound strategic logic requires its continuation. Committing to enlargement is to commit to establishing NATO as *the* central vehicle for building a stable Europe. To halt its expansion at Poland's eastern border therefore makes no strategic sense. Instead, NATO must set its sights on drawing Russia itself into the alliance.

Three Reasons for Russia's Inclusion

NATO should follow this course for three reasons. First, Russian inclusion is a condition for a durable peace. A central determinant of European stability in coming decades, perhaps *the* central determinant, will be whether Russia exercises its power in a benign or malign manner. During the critical period in Russia's transition from its present disorder to reassuming natural weight, the West should be doing all it can to support democratic reform and to expose Russians to the norms and attitudes that underpin the responsible conduct of foreign policy—tasks best accomplished with Russia inside, rather than excluded from, the NATO tent.

Second, integrating Russia into NATO will prevent the emergence of a new gray zone in the heart of Europe. Those states that lie between an enlarged NATO and Russia—the Baltics, Slovakia, Romania, Bulgaria, Moldova, Belarus, Ukraine—remain Europe's most fragile and vulnerable members. To halt NATO enlargement after the first wave would only exacerbate their security predicament. To the extent that any sort of strategic vision now exists among NATO members, it calls for the elimination of this gray zone through successive waves of NATO enlargement. But admitting these states into NATO sequentially from west to east would surely have the dangerous end result of isolating Russia. However much it is reassured about NATO's benign intentions, Russia should not and would not stand by idly as every country on its western flank joins an opposing military bloc.

Third, Russia's entry into NATO would give the Atlantic community more influence over developments in Europe's east, where the key challenges of the coming decades will arise. At stake are the security of Russia's nuclear weapons and technology, Russia's relationship with China, the stability of Ukraine, and access to Caspian oil—interests that warrant deep Western engagement. Russia's relationship with its smaller neighbors, too, would be subject to the restraining effects of NATO's cooperative rules, helping to eliminate the residue of imperial ambition. In contrast, halting NATO enlargement at the frontier between Poland and Belarus would restrict the alliance from engaging in those parts of Europe where its peace-causing effects are most needed.

Clinton Administration

The Clinton administration, at least to judge by its rhetoric, has not ruled out Russia's eventual membership in NATO. In the President's [Bill Clinton's] words, "NATO's doors will remain open to all those willing to shoulder the responsibilities of membership." In reality, though, most officials do not take seriously the notion of Russian membership. At best, the minority willing to entertain the idea puts Russia at the end of a long queue, behind all the countries to its West.

Russia should be moved close to the front of the queue. To buy time for Russian democracy to deepen and for its economy to recover and mature, a small second wave of enlargement, one not likely to provoke Russia (Slovenia, Austria and Romania are prime candidates), should begin immediately. But the third wave should include Russia—so long as its economic and political circumstances improve—perhaps even accompanied by its three Baltic neighbors. Barring the collapse of the reform process, 2010 would seem a reasonable target date for Russia's entry into NATO.

Three Objections

The proposal to integrate Russia into NATO faces three main objections: that Russia is not interested in NATO membership; that Russia is headed toward collapse; and that Russia's entry into NATO would fundamentally alter the character of the alliance.

As to the first objection, Moscow remains uninterested in joining NATO in large part because it continues to see the alliance as an anti-Russian organization. This perception stems from NATO's persistence as a traditional military alliance and its purposeful aggregation of capability against—who else?—Russia. Were NATO to redefine its core mission and make clear its intention to include Russia, Russian perceptions of the alliance would evolve accordingly.

Brian Duffy. Reprinted with special permission of King Features Syndicate.

While the claim that Russian reform has veered off track has substance, it is far too soon to write Russia off. On the contrary, there are three potent reasons to remain cautiously optimistic about Russia's future and hence to entertain seriously the notion that it will be ready to join NATO within a decade.

Russia Is Not Coming Apart

First, Russia is not coming apart at the seams. Although the country's regions are growing more powerful at the expense of the central government, devolution, on balance, contributes to the stability and integrity of the country. The strengthening of regional governors has brought a definitive end to the authoritarian state. In certain regions, democratic accountability, interest group formation, pluralist debate, entrepreneurship and market development are faring much better than at the national level. Indeed, these wealthier and more progressive regions may well emerge as the anchors of a decentralized Russian state.

Although the central government has lost its power more by default than by design, devolution will not soon become fragmentation. Moscow retains control of the military. It also remains the country's financial center, to which regional governments and firms turn for subsidies and capital. And if residents in the regions want more autonomy, most do not wish for independence. Ethnic Russians, who comprise roughly 82 percent of the population, remain firmly committed to an integral state.

Second, democracy and civil society, although still primitive, have begun to take root throughout Russia. Elections are today a matter of course. Voters choose from numerous candidates whose views range across the political spectrum. The media are relatively free and open debate the norm. Needless to say, Russia is not yet a liberal democracy. But there are good reasons to believe that the liberalizing forces that have swept from Europe's west to its east will with time take firmer hold.

Third, Russia is no longer an adversary of the West. It poses no military threat whatsoever to Central or Western Europe. Even ardent nationalists recognize that Central Europe has departed the Russian sphere. Although Russia has at times exercised its influence in the near abroad through coercive means, it has by no means attempted to reconstitute an imperial zone of domination. And to the extent that it barks at all, Russia's bark is much worse than its bite. Russia and China decry American hegemony, but do next to nothing to impede it. Despite confrontational rhetoric over NATO expansion, Iraq and the Balkans, Moscow has for the most part acceded to Western policy. Even while it condemned NATO's intervention in Yugoslavia and deployed a symbolic naval vessel to the Mediterranean, Russia continued to honor the arms embargo against Yugoslavia and kept its troops in NATO's peacekeeping operation in Bosnia. Far from being an intractable adversary, Russia is at worst a prickly bystander—and at times a reluctant but, as the Kosovo crisis shows, a very useful partner.

Transforming NATO

It is true, of course, that Russian membership in NATO would dilute the alliance and alter its character. But in the absence of an external threat, NATO must transform itself if it is to remain relevant. Its focus on defending the territory of members needs to give way to an emphasis on peacekeeping and on deepening cooperation among former adversaries. Automatic and binding defense guarantees should be replaced by more informal commitments to protect common interests through common action. If NATO is to be a vehicle for building security across Europe, it should cease drawing new lines and focus instead on integrating all of Europe's democracies into a cooperative security community.

Periodical Bibliography

The following articles have been selected to supplement the diverse views presented in this chapter. Addresses are provided for periodicals not indexed in the *Readers' Guide to Periodical Literature*, the *Alternative Press Index*, the *Social Sciences Index*, or the *Index to Legal Periodicals and Books*.

Zbigniew Brzezinski — "Bombshells Lurk in the Russian Scandal," *Wall Street Journal*, September 3, 1999.

Paolo Cotta-Ramusino — "The Unasked Question," *Bulletin of the Atomic Scientists*, July/August 1999.

James M. Goldgeiger — "The U.S. Decision to Enlarge: How, When, Why, and What Next?" *Brookings Review*, Summer 1999.

Anatol Lieven — "A New Iron Curtain," *Atlantic Monthly*, January 1996.

Thomas W. Lippmann and Helen Dewar — "Who Says Bipartisanship Is Dead?" *Washington Post National Weekly Edition*, March 16, 1998. Available from Reprints, 1150 15th St. NW, Washington, DC 20071.

Igor Maslov — "Russia and NATO: A Critical Period," *Mediterranean Quarterly*, Winter 1998. Available from Duke University Press, Box 90660, Durham, NC 27708-0660.

Michael McFaul — "Russia's Pyrrhic 'Pristina Victory,'" *Wall Street Journal*, June 18, 1999.

Walter Russell Mead — "Whose Russia to Lose?" *Los Angeles Times*, September 12, 1999. Available from Reprints, Times Mirror Square, Los Angeles, CA 90053.

James Oberg — "NASA's Russian Payload," *American Spectator*, August 1998.

Robert E. Rubin — "Don't Give Up on Russia," *New York Times*, September 21, 1999.

Katrina vanden Heuvel — "Russia and Election 2000," *Nation*, September 6–13, 1999.

Charles Weiss Jr. — "Eurasia Letter: A Marshall Plan We Can Afford," *Foreign Policy*, Spring 1997.

Fareed Zakaria — "Can't Russia Join the Club, Too?" *Newsweek*, May 4, 1998.

For Further Discussion

Chapter 1

1. How much are David M. Kotz and Virginia Postrel in agreement over the effects of the "shock therapy" programs Russia enacted with Western assistance and guidance? What is the crux of their differing views on these programs? What alternative policies do Kotz and Postrel propose?

2. David Hoffman, Gary T. Dempsey, and Aaron Lukas all utilize anecdotes about the personal experiences of themselves and of Russians in their articles about crime and corruption in Russia. What purposes do such anecdotes perform, in your view? Do they lend a special credence to the authors' respective arguments? Explain.

3. Murray Feshbach argues that people who analyze Russia's problems must take into consideration fundamental demographic realities about its shrinking population. Can you conceive how Russia's health problems might affect the nation's long-term military, economic, and geopolitical status? Explain.

Chapter 2

1. Does Leon Aron acknowledge some of the problems of Russia's government that Aleksandr Solzhenitsyn focuses on? If so, why is he more optimistic than Solzhenitsyn about the future of Russia's democracy?

2. What aspects of Russian society make democracy difficult, according to W. Bruce Lincoln? Do Alexander Elder or Leon Aron provide convincing examples of societal evolution toward democracy in Russia, in your opinion? Explain.

3. Alexander Elder and Aleksandr Solzhenitsyn were both at one time political refugees of the old Soviet Union. Does their past status as refugees, in your opinion, give greater authority to their present pronouncements on Russia compared to foreigners such as W. Bruce Lincoln? Defend your answer.

Chapter 3

1. Henry A. Kissinger argues that Russia's foreign policy is motivated by a hunger for "prestige." What examples and arguments does he provide to support his claim? Do you find Sestanovich's analysis debunking "prestige" as a motivating factor in Russia more or less convincing than Kissinger's arguments? Explain your answer.

2. William C. Martel argues that there is no conclusive evidence

that nuclear weapons or materials have "leaked" from Russia. Assuming he is correct, does the absence of such evidence, in your view, provide sufficient reassurance against the concerns raised by Steve Goldstein? Why or why not?

3. How do James O. Finckenauer and Elin J. Waring define the term "mafia" in their analysis of whether a Russian mafia exists in the United States? Do you think their definition is useful? Is their understanding of what the word means different from that of Steven Handelman and James Kim in their respective viewpoints? Explain your answer.

Chapter 4

1. At the close of his article, Jacob Heilbrun, who has identified Strobe Talbott as the "architect" of U.S. policy on Russia under President Bill Clinton, decries the "Talbottian formula" as "give, give, give." After reading the two viewpoints by Heilbrun and Talbott, do you believe Heilbrun's characterization of U.S.-Russian policy under Talbott is accurate or fair? Why or why not?

2. Do Charles A. Kupchan's arguments in favor of including Russia in NATO more closely agree with those of Gary Hart and Gordon Humphrey (opposing NATO expansion in Europe) or with those of Ariel Cohen (favoring it)? Explain your answer.

Organizations to Contact

The editors have compiled the following list of organizations concerned with issues debated in this book. The descriptions are derived from materials provided by the organizations. All have publications or information available for interested readers. The list was compiled on the date of publication of the present volume; the information provided here may change. Be aware that many organizations take several weeks or longer to respond to inquiries, so allow as much time as possible.

American Enterprise Institute for Public Policy Research (AEI)
1150 17th St. NW, Washington, DC 20036
(202) 862-5800 • fax: (202) 862-7177
e-mail: dmaxwell@aei.org • website: www.aei.org

AEI is a conservative think tank that studies national and international issues. It publishes *Russian Outlook*, a periodic report and analysis on Russian affairs.

American Foreign Policy Council (AFPC)
1521 16th St. NW, Washington, DC 20036
e-mail: afpc@afpc.org • website: www.afpc.org

The AFPC produces and disseminates reports and analyses on global affairs. It publishes numerous reports and analyses in its *Russia Reform Monitor* and in monographs and studies.

Brookings Institution
1775 Massachusetts Ave. NW, Washington, DC 20036
(202) 797-6000 • fax: (202) 797-6004
website: www.brook.edu

The institution is a liberal research and education organization that publishes material on economics, government, and foreign policy. It strives to serve as a bridge between scholarship and public policy, bringing new knowledge to the attention of decision makers and providing scholars with improved insight into public policy issues. Its publications include the quarterly *Brookings Review* and books including *Russia's Virtual Economy*.

Cato Institute
1000 Massachusetts Ave. NW, Washington, DC 20001-5403
(202) 842-0200 • fax: (202) 842-3490
e-mail: cato@cato.org • website: www.cato.org

The Cato Institute is a libertarian public policy research foundation dedicated to limiting the control of government and stimulating foreign policy debate. It publishes occasional materials on Russia in its triennial *Cato Journal*, the bimonthly newsletter *Cato Policy Report*, and the periodic *Cato Policy Analysis*.

Center for Citizen Initiatives
Presidio of San Francisco
Building 1008, General Kennedy Ave.
PO Box 29912, San Francisco, CA 94129-0912
(415) 561-7777 • fax: (415) 561-7778
e-mail: info@ccisf.org • website: http://ccisf.org

The center, formerly the Center for U.S.-USSR Initiatives, works to strengthen relations between Americans and the peoples of the former Soviet republics. It sponsors agricultural, environmental, and economic programs to assist the republics in creating better societies. The center publishes three bimonthly newsletters and a variety of brochures.

Center for Strategic and International Studies (CSIS)
1800 K St. NW, Washington, DC 20006
(202) 887-0200 • fax: (202) 775-3199
website: www.csis.org

CSIS is a public policy research institution. Its Russian and Eurasian Program provides information and analyses on political and economic developments in Russia and other states of the former Soviet Union. The Center's publications include the *Washington Quarterly* and *Expert Briefs*.

Council on Foreign Relations (CFR)
58 E. 68th St., New York, NY 10021
(212) 734-0400
website: www.foreignrelations.org

The council is a group of individuals with specialized knowledge of foreign affairs. It was formed to study the international aspects of American political and economic policies and problems. Articles on Russia are published in its journal *Foreign Affairs* and on its website.

Foreign Policy Association (FPA)
470 Park Ave. South, New York, NY 10016-6819
(212) 481-8100
website: www.fpa.org

The association is an educational organization that provides nonpartisan information to help citizens participate in foreign policy decisions. Articles on Russia are often featured in its publications, which include the *Headline Series* of analyses and the annual *Great Decisions*.

Heritage Foundation
214 Massachusetts Ave. NE, Washington, DC 20002-4999
(202) 546-4400 • fax: (202) 546-8328
e-mail: info@heritage.org • website: www.heritage.org

The foundation is a conservative public policy research institute dedicated to the principles of free, competitive enterprise, limited government, and individual liberty. Its scholars write numerous articles on Russia and related foreign policy issues that are published in the quarterly *Policy Review*, as well as in monographs, books, and background papers.

Hudson Institute
Herman Kahn Center
5395 Emerson Way, Indianapolis, IN 46226
(317) 545-1000 • fax: (317) 545-9639
e-mail: info@hudson.org • website: www.hudson.org

The institute studies public policy aspects of national and international economics. Publications include the the *American Outlook Magazine*, research papers, and books such as *Commonwealth or Empire?*

Institute for Policy Studies
733 15th St. NW, Suite 1020, Washington, DC 20005-2112
(202) 234-9382 • fax: (202) 387-7915
e-mail: scott@hotsalsa.org • website: www.ips-dc.org

The institute's national security program provides factual analyses and critiques of America's foreign policies. Its goal is to provide a balanced view of international relations. The institute publishes books, reports, and briefs.

International Foundation for Election Systems (IFES)
121099 Russia, Moscow, B. Strochenovsky Per. 15A
(095) 232-3820
e-mail: ifes@ifes.ru • website: www.ifes.ru:8101

The IFES, funded primarily by the U.S. Agency for International Development, is dedicated to promoting fair and credible elections in Russia. It provides technical assistance and training and works in cooperation with Russian nongovernment organizations and election commissions. Its website includes numerous articles and commentaries on electoral law and democracy in Russia.

National Committee on American Foreign Policy
320 Park Ave., 8th Floor, New York, NY 10022
(212) 224-1120 • fax: (212) 224-2524
e-mail: ncafp@aol.com • website: www.ncafp.org

The committee is composed of Americans from varied backgrounds who are interested in foreign policy and want to encourage citizen participation in foreign policy decisions. It also organizes fact-finding missions that meet with top political and economic leaders. Publications include the bimonthly *American Foreign Policy-Newsletter*, monographs, and books.

Permanent Mission of the Russian Federation to the United Nations
136 East 67 St., New York, NY 10021
(212) 861-4900 • fax: (212) 628-0252
website: www.un.int/russia

The resident office of Russia's United Nations representative releases official statements and press releases from various government ministries on human rights, Russian foreign affairs, and other matters. Much of this material is available on its website.

Reason Foundation
3415 S. Sepulveda Blvd., Suite 400, Los Angeles, CA 90034
(310) 391-2245
website: www.reason.org

The foundation promotes individual freedoms and free-market principles. It has published articles on Russia and U.S. foreign policy in its monthly *Reason* magazine, newsletters, research reports, and books.

U.S. Department of State
Office of Public Communications, Public Information Service
Bureau of Public Affairs, Washington, DC 20520
(202) 647-6575
website: www.state.gov

The Department of State advises the president on the formulation and execution of foreign policy. It publishes speeches and testimonies by government officials. It features numerous articles on Russia and on NATO in its website.

World Policy Institute
777 United Nations Plaza, New York, NY 10017
(212) 490-0010
website: http://worldpolicy.org
The institute, affiliated with the New School for Social Research in New York City, is a public policy research organization that studies national security issues and foreign affairs. Publications of the institute include the quarterly *World Policy Journal*, books, monographs, and pamphlets.

Websites

Russia on the Net
www.ru
Russia on the Net is an electronic directory, similar to Yahoo and other portals, created and maintained in Russia. It provides a listing of Internet sites from and about Russia and other former Soviet states.

Russia Today
www.russiatoday.com
This site offers an online version of the daily English language newspaper that includes past and present articles on the Russian Federation, political commentary, and economic reporting.

Bibliography of Books

Mikhail A. Alexseev, ed. *Center-Periphery Conflict in Post-Soviet Russia: A Federation Imperiled.* New York: St. Martin's Press, 1999.

Wayne Allensworth *The Russian Question: Nationalism, Modernization, and Post-Communist Russia.* Lanham, MD: Rowman & Littlefield, 1997.

Graham T. Allison *Avoiding Nuclear Anarchy: Containing the Threat of Loose Russian Nuclear Weapons and Fissile Material.* Cambridge, MA: MIT Press, 1996.

Alexei Arbatov et al., eds. *Managing Conflict in the Former Soviet Union: Russian and American Perspectives.* Cambridge, MA: MIT Press, 1997.

Adele Marie Barker, ed. *Consuming Russia: Popular Culture, Sex, and Society Since Gorbachev.* Durham, NC: Duke University Press, 1999.

Rose Brady *Kapitalizm: Russia's Struggle to Free Its Economy.* New Haven, CT: Yale University Press, 1999.

Mary Buckley, ed. *Post-Soviet Women.* New York: Cambridge University Press, 1997.

Ted Galen Carpenter and Barbara Conry, eds. *NATO Enlargement: Illusions and Reality.* Washington, DC: Cato Institute, 1998.

Glen E. Curtis, ed. *Russia: A Country Study.* Washington, DC: U.S. Government Printing Office, 1998.

Judith Devlin *Slavophiles and Commissars: Enemies of Democracy in Modern Russia.* New York: St. Martin's Press, 1999.

Susan Eisenhower, ed. *NATO at Fifty: Perspectives on the Future of the Transatlantic Alliance.* Washington, DC: Center for Political and Strategic Studies, 1999.

Stephen Handelman *Comrade Criminal: Russia's New Mafiya.* New Haven, CT: Yale University Press, 1995.

Timothy Harper *Moscow Madness: Crime, Corruption, and One Man's Pursuit of Profit in the New Russia.* New York : McGraw-Hill, 1999.

Gregory Ioff and Tatyana Nefedova *Continuity and Change in Rural Russia.* Boulder, CO: Westview Press, 1997.

Heyward Isham, ed. *Remaking Russia.* Armonk, NY: M.E. Sharpe, 1995.

N.O. Kura, ed. *Russia at Crossroads: Prosperity or Abyss?* Commack, NY: Nova Science, 1999.

Stanislav Lunev	*Through the Eyes of the Enemy: Russia's Highest Ranking Military Defector Reveals Why Russia Is More Dangerous Than Ever*. Washington, DC: Regnery, 1998.
Tim McDaniel	*The Agony of the Russian Idea*. Princeton, NJ: Princeton University Press, 1996.
Dmitry Mikheyev	*Russia Transformed*. Indianapolis, IN: Hudson Institute, 1996.
Joseph L. Nogee and R. Judson Mitchell	*Russian Politics: The Struggle for a New Order*. Needham Heights, MA: Allyn and Bacon, 1997.
Nicolai N. Petro	*The Rebirth of Russian Democracy*. Cambridge, MA: Harvard University Press, 1995.
David Remnick	*Resurrection: The Struggle for a New Russia*. New York: Random House, 1997.
Wilma Rule and Norma C. Noonan, eds.	*Russian Women in Politics and Society*. Westport, CT: Greenwood Press, 1996.
Victor Sergeyev	*The Wild East: Crime and Lawlessness in Post-Communist Russia*. Armonk, NY: M.E. Sharpe, 1998.
Lilia Shevtsova	*Yeltsin's Russia: Myths and Reality*. Washington, DC: Carnegie Endowment for International Peace, 1999.
Dimitri K. Simes	*After the Collapse: Russia Seeks Its Place as a Great Power*. New York: Simon & Schuster, 1999.
Gordon B. Smith, ed.	*State-Building in Russia: The Yeltsin Legacy and the Challenge of the Future*. Armonk, NY: M.E. Sharpe, 1999.
Alexander Solzhenitsyn	*The Russian Question*. Translated and annotated by Yermolai Solzhenitsyn. New York: Farrar, Straus and Giroux, 1995.
Mark Taplin	*Open Lands: Travels Through Russia's Once Forbidden Places*. South Royalton, VT: Steerforth Press, 1997.
Henry Trofimenko	*Russian National Interests and the Current Crisis in Russia*. Brookfield, VT: Ashgate, 1999.
Phil Williams, ed.	*Russian Organized Crime: The New Threat?* Portland, OR: Frank Cass, 1997.
Daniel Yergin and Thane Gustafson	*Russia 2010: And What It Means for the World*. New York: Random House, 1993.
Gennady Zyuganov	*My Russia*. Armonk, NY: M.E. Sharpe, 1997.

Index

Abadinsky, Howard, 142
Abkhazia, 130
ABM Treaty, 169
Abraham Lincoln and the Second American Revolution (McPherson), 81
acid rain, 55
AIDS/HIV, 60–61
air pollution, 52–55, 56–57
Albright, David, 128
Albright, Madeleine, 153, 155
  on democracy in Russia, 79
Alexander II, 85
al Qaeda (terrorist organization), 127, 129
Anderson, Scott, 145
Andrakhanova, Olga, 57
Antigua, 142
Armenia, 109
Armey, Dick, 74
Aron, Leon, 73
Asian financial crisis, 22
Aslun, Anders, 37
Atlantic Alliance, 110, 111
Aum Shinri Kyo, 129
autocracy
  reform under, 84–85
  under the tsars, 91–92
Azerbaijan, 109

Balkans, the, 167–68
Bank Imperil, 163
Bank of New York, 37, 141–42
Baranovski, Igor, 45
Belkin, Victor, 31
Benzovsky, Boris, 39
Blank, Stephen, 107
Bogomolov, Oleg, 29
Boldyrev, Yuri, 37
Bolshevik Revolution, 14
Brighton Beach, 147
Brovkin, Vladimir, 142, 143
Brzezinski, Zbigniew, 120, 121, 123
Bunn, Matthew, 127
Bush, George, 122
businesses
  during Soviet oppression, 93
  law enforcement for, 43
  laws on private, 95–96
  organized crime in, 30–31, 39, 44–45, 46–47, 137–38
  propping of industrial, 32–33

Camdessus, Michel, 164
capitalism
  causing economic decline, 23, 28–29
  and crime, 42
  failure of, 74
  organized crime as threat to, 47–48
  Russia adopting a pretend, 29–33
  Russian opinion on, 76–77
Catherine the Great, 85
Chechen war
  Clinton justifying, 106
  IMF loans funding, 164
  nuclear materials used in, 129
Chernomyrdin, Viktor, 161, 163
China
  economy of, compared with Russia, 31–32, 180
  nuclear scientists in, 132–33
  relations with Russia, 110
chlamydia, 61
Chubais, Anatoly B., 71–72, 163
Cilluffo, Frank, 141, 143
clear-cutting, 55
Clinton, Bill
  on Chechen war, 106
  infidelities of, 28, 29
  loans to Russia under, 22, 165
  on NATO inclusion of Russia, 184
  Russian foreign policy under, 105, 110, 161–62
  treatment of Russian leaders, 122
  see also United States
coal
  pollution from, 50–51, 53–55
Cohen, Ariel, 176
Cohen, Stephen, 65
Collision and Collusion (Wedel), 163
Colombian drug lords, 142
Commonwealth of Independent States (CIS), 117, 169
communism
  brutal repression by, 91–94
  civic responsibility destroyed by, 87–89
  collapse of, 94–96
  corruption under, 80, 157
  coup attempts by, 96–98
  downfall of, 15
  in 1995 election, 77
  in 1996 election, 68, 77, 98–99
  and patriotism, 114
  will not return, 99–100
  vs. Yeltsin, 116–17
contract killings, 39
Cooperative Threat Reduction program, 133, 134
corruption. *See* organized crime
Council on Foreign and Defense

Policy (CFDP), 118–20
crime. *See* mafia (Russian); organized crime
Czechoslovakia, 96
 see also NATO expansion

de Borchgrave, Arnaud, 45
democracy in Russia
 communism destroying civic responsibility for, 87–89
 coup attempts resisting, 96–98
 distorted view of, 81–82
 does not exist, 67–68
 evolution toward, 105–106
 failure of, 74
 has not taken root, 88
 historical opposition to, 84–86
 as irreversible, 99
 new freedoms through, 78–79
 obstacles to, 65
 vs. oligarchy, 69–71
 staged elections, 68–69
 turning away from, 89
 Western view of, 67
 see also reform
Dempsey, Gary T., 41
de Soto, Hernando, 30
Dmitriyev, Yuri, 36, 39, 40
Dmitriyeva, Tatyana, 60

Eberstadt, Nicholas, 61
economic crisis, 19
 alternative strategies for overcoming, 24–26
 causes
  capitalism, 28–29
  fall of pre-existing economy, 23–24
 International Monetary Fund's influence, 21–22
 low gross national product, 31–32
 and neoliberalism, 26
 and nuclear proliferation, 126, 127
 organized crime worsening, 72
 propping industrial businesses, 32–33
 stifling private enterprise, 29–31
economic reform
 failure of, 71–72, 74
 improvements from, 76
 Russian economy before, 75
 see also economic crisis
Edelshtein, Father Georgi, 164
Elder, Alexander, 90
elections
 increase in, 78, 155
 1996, 65, 68–69, 77, 98
 reformers as winners in, 99
 staged, 68–69
 2000, 65

unfair, 71
employment. *See* wages
environmental crisis, 50
 acid rain, 55
 air pollution, 52–55
 health problems from, 56–57, 59
 lack of government action on, 57
 laws on, 57
 nuclear waste dumping, 55
 oil spills, 55
 pollution in Kuzbass, 50–51
 water pollution, 51–52
Ermarth, Fritz, 74
Estonia, 172

Fainberg, Ludwig, 143
Feshbach, Murray, 57, 58
financial crisis. *See* economic crisis
Finckenauer, James O., 144, 147
foreign policy (Russian)
 alliance with Iran, 166–67
 on the Balkans, 167–68
 expansionism, 107–109
  con, 115–17
 as imperialistic, 107
  con, 117–20
 is not obsessed with prestige, 120–22
 lack of U.S. response to, 110–11
 quest for power, 107
 U.S. coddling Yeltsin, 105–106, 111
  con, 122–24
 see also NATO expansion
Founding Act on Relations between Russia and NATO, 178–79
freedom of the press, 67
FREEDOM Support Act, 154–55
 budget cuts for, 159
Freeh, Louis, 142
free market economy. *See* capitalism
Friendly, Alfred, 57

Gaddy, Clifford, 32
Gaidar, Yegor T., 71–72, 110, 178
Galeotti, Mark, 36
Garelik, Glenn, 49
Garrett, Laurie, 60
Genghis Khan, 91
Georgia, 130
Germany, 96, 124
glasnost, 85, 94
Goldstein, Steve, 125
Gorbachev, Mikhail, 85
 loss of power, 97
 reforms by, 14–15, 71–72, 94
 under house arrest, 96
Gore, Al, 110, 161, 164
government
 on environmental crisis, 57

Russia

DATE DUE

APR 2 7 2004			
APR 0 3 2006			
NOV 2 6 2008			